Basic KNITTING

All the Skills and Tools You Need to Get Started

Leigh Ann Berry, editor

*Anita J. Tosten and Missy Burns,
knitters and consultants*

*Photographs by
Alan Wycheck*

*Illustrations by
Marjorie Leggitt*

STACKPOLE
BOOKS

Copyright © 2004 by Stackpole Books

Published by
STACKPOLE BOOKS
5067 Ritter Road
Mechanicsburg, PA 17055
www.stackpolebooks.com

Printed in China

10 9 8 7 6 5 4

FIRST EDITION

Photographs by Alan Wycheck
Illustrations by Marjorie Leggitt
Cover design by Tracy Patterson

All patterns © Anita J. Tosten

Library of Congress Cataloging-in-Publication Data

Basic knitting : all the skills and tools you need to get started/
Leigh Ann Berry, editor ; Anita J. Tosten and Missy Burns,
knitters and consultants ; photographs by Alan Wycheck ;
illustrations by Marjorie Leggitt.— 1st ed.
        p. cm.
ISBN 0-8117-3109-X
1. Knitting. 2. Knitting—Patterns. I. Berry, Leigh Ann.
TT820 .B367 2004
746.43'2—dc22
                                                    2003015108

ISBN 978-0-8117-3109-6

Contents

Acknowledgments

Editing this book has truly been a labor of love. Many people have helped and encouraged me along the way:

Carol Woolcock, of The Mannings in East Berlin, Pennsylvania, whose generosity and helpfulness allowed us to photograph yarn, needles, and knitting accessories. The Mannings is one of the most comprehensive knitting stores in the region, and Carol's openness with her inventory enabled us to photograph a wide array of tools and supplies.

My Stackpole colleague, Susan Drexler, whose own passion for knitting helped to inspire my own. Sharing new yarns and projects in progress with someone who can truly appreciate them is one of the joys of being a knitter.

Garrick Chow, who patiently tolerated my incessant ramblings about knitting and accompanied me as I dragged him to knitting stores from Pennsylvania to California. Only the partner of a knitting addict can appreciate the extent of the obsession.

Photographer Alan Wycheck, who provided invaluable advice and guidance in addition to his exceptional photographic ability. His unfailing commitment to thoroughness and quality has helped to make this book as complete as I hope beginning knitters will find it to be.

Finally, Anita Tosten and Missy Burns, who provided the vision and creative inspiration for this endeavor. Anita's talents as a designer are showcased in the 10 projects included in the book. I feel truly blessed to have had the opportunity to collaborate with two of the most talented, hardest-working women in the business. In addition to teaching and designing, Anita and Missy manage Wool in the Woods, a young but thriving company that produces some of the beautiful hand-dyed yarn featured in these pages. Their enthusiasm and sense of humor have made this project a true pleasure for me. Special thanks to Anita and her husband, Rod, for allowing us to photograph the finished projects in and around their home; and to Missy's daughter, Megan Dupont, who served as our model for the finished garments.

—Leigh Ann Berry

Introduction

Knitting is a craft that is presently enjoying a renaissance of sorts. Around the world, people young and old are discovering—or rediscovering—the joy of working with needles and yarn. First practiced in ancient times, hand knitting has evolved from a necessary means of producing socks and stockings into a craft that is limited only by a knitter's creativity.

This book is intended to serve as a comprehensive introduction to the basic skills you will need to master in order to become a knitter. The focus of the first half of the book is on detailed, step-by-step text and photo sequences that will teach you how to execute the basic stitches and techniques of knitting. The second half of the book will show you how to apply these basic skills when completing actual projects. The skill workshops that accompany each project will teach you skills and techniques that are relevant to a particular piece or garment. A few of the projects also include "Project in Progress" sections, which show you the more complex stages of the project in step-by-step detail.

We recommend that you spend your first hours with this book in the Basic Skills section, learning and mastering the fundamental stitches and techniques. Then, once you are comfortable working with needles and yarn, you can move on to try one of the ten projects included in the second half of the book. The first project, the Teddy Bear Sweater, offers a good first project to put these skills to use, and we suggest that you attempt this project first before moving on to any of the others. Working a sweater in miniature allows you to practice the same techniques you will need to use in later projects. The Skill Workshops that accompany this project also teach finishing techniques that will be required for other garments later in the book.

So pick up your needles and yarn and get ready to learn how to knit!

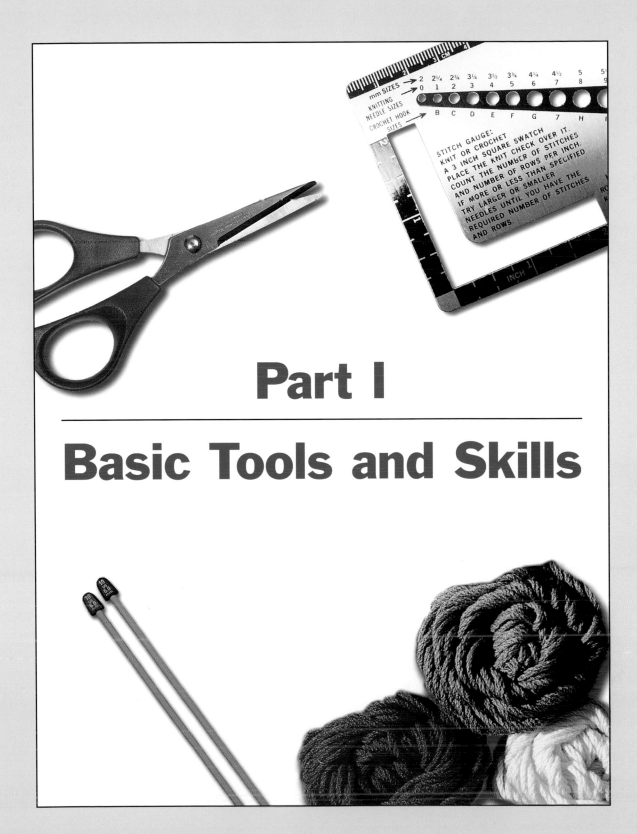

Part I

Basic Tools and Skills

Yarn

COLOR

Yarn comes in as many colors as the rainbow: reds, oranges, yellows, greens, blues, indigos, and violets and every shade in between. Variegated yarns combine several complementary colors into one multi-hued skein.

Most yarn is dyed commercially in batches, or lots. The color of these batches can vary from one to another and the differences in color will become obvious when switching from one skein to another in a knitted garment. To avoid any potential color discrepancies, make sure to purchase enough yarn to complete your project all at once, making sure to check the skeins' labels to ensure that the dye lot number is the same.

Your local knitting store offers yarn in as many colors, weights, and textures as you can imagine.

The CYCA's 6 yarn weight categories (from top to bottom): Super Fine, Fine, Light, Medium, Bulky, and Super Bulky.

WEIGHT

Yarn also comes in a range of different weights. From the super fine yarn that is perfect for knitting soft, delicate baby blankets up to the super bulky wool used to knit thick, heavy sweaters, a yarn's weight has a great impact on the finished knitted product. Typically, when you knit a project from a pattern, it will specify the type of yarn to be used. In order to complete the project as the designer intended, it is important to conform to the suggested yarn weight or, if making a substitution, to come as close as possible to the recommended knit gauge. If, however, you are designing your own garment, a knowledge of the various yarn weights will help you to select a yarn that is most appropriate to the finished garment you are preparing to knit.

In order to provide a measure of consistency in yarn labeling, the Craft Yarn Council of America (CYCA) has issued a set of standards dealing with yarn weight. The guidelines organize yarn into 6 main weight categories ranging from Super Fine (1) up to Super Bulky (6). In between are Fine (2), Light (3), Medium (4), and Bulky (5). See the appendix on page 118 for all the details on this relatively new organizational structure.

COMPOSITION AND STRUCTURE

The vast majority of knitting yarn is created by spinning fibers together. Fibers can be natural, such as wool, mohair, silk, or cotton; man-made, such as acrylic, nylon, or polyester; or a blend of the two. Each fiber has its own distinctive characteristics and properties, some of which are desirable and others which are less so. Wool, for example, is extremely warm, but is not as strong as other fibers. Acrylic, on the other hand, is extremely durable but does not breathe well. Sometimes a blend of the two materials maximizes the advantages of each. For example, a sock yarn made of a 92% wool and 8% acrylic blend provides the warmth and comfort of natural wool with the added strength and resilience of synthetic fiber.

The way in which the yarn's fibers are spun together determines its structure. There are a variety of different yarn structures:

Spiral: A thinner yarn twisted around a thicker yarn.

Chenille: A velvety pile, wrapped with two thin, twisted threads. Can be either long-pile or short-pile.

Boucle: Two strands twisted at varying tensions, held together with a thin binding thread to produce loops of yarn.

Nubby: Two strands twisted so that one overlaps another to produce a bumpy texture.

Slubby: A strand that is alternately thick and thin, twisted with either a smooth or a slubby second strand.

Tape: Yarn made of knitted threads and woven into a narrow, flat band.

Novelty Yarns: Most common types combine metallic threads or feature long "eyelash" textures.

Z AND S TWIST

A yarn with a Z twist (left) has twists turning upward and to the right while an S twist (right) has twists turning upward and to the left.

4

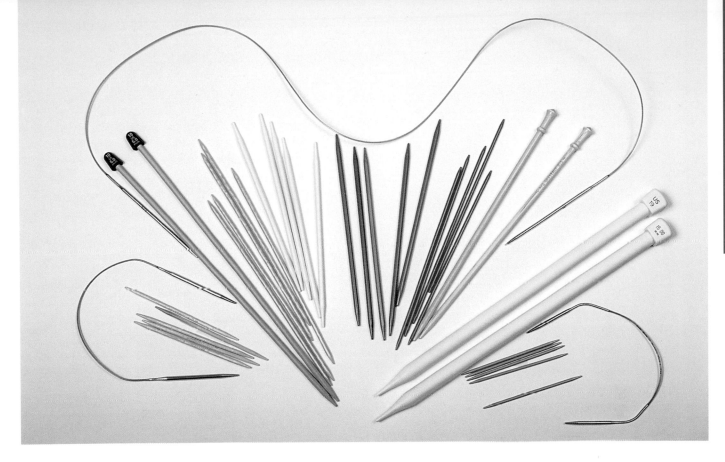

Knitting Needle Sizes*

Millimeter Range	U.S. Size Range
2.25 mm	1
2.75 mm	2
3.25 mm	3
3.5 mm	4
3.75 mm	5
4 mm	6
4.5 mm	7
5 mm	8
5.5 mm	9
6 mm	10
6.5 mm	10$^1/_2$
8 mm	11
9 mm	13
10 mm	15
12.75 mm	17
15 mm	19
19 mm	35
25 mm	50

*From the Craft Yarn Council of America's Standards and Guidelines for Crochet and Knitting

Needles

Aside from yarn, the knitting needle is the knitter's fundamental tool. Needles come in three main varieties: straight, circular, or double pointed. They range in both length and size from a 2.25 mm size 1 needle up to a 25 mm size 50 needle.

Needles come in a range of different materials: aluminum, steel, plastic, bamboo, or wood. The last two materials are typically more expensive but can be more pleasurable to knit with.

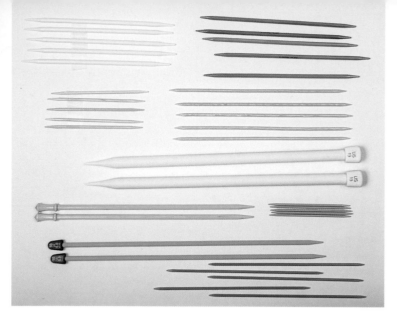

STRAIGHT NEEDLES

Most knitters start off using straight needles; they are the simplest and most straightforward tool a knitter has to get the job done. Typically, straight needles are used to knit back and forth across a flat piece of knitting. Straight needles come in lengths ranging from 8 to 16 inches. Most small beginning projects such as scarves or children's garments are best completed on 10-inch needles, but larger projects such as adult sweaters require a 16-inch needle to accommodate all the stitches.

CIRCULAR NEEDLES

Circular needles are typically used when knitting in the round. Knitting on circular needles produces a seamless, tubular piece of knitting, perfect when creating a hat or the body of a sweater. Circular needles come in various sizes: 12, 16, 20, 24, 32, and 40-inch lengths are available. Always use the length of needle that your pattern indicates. Knitting on a longer needle than is indicated will stretch the stitches and distort the final piece. Circular needles can also be used in place of straight needles to do flat knitting by simply turning the work from right to wrong side rather than knitting in the round (see box below).

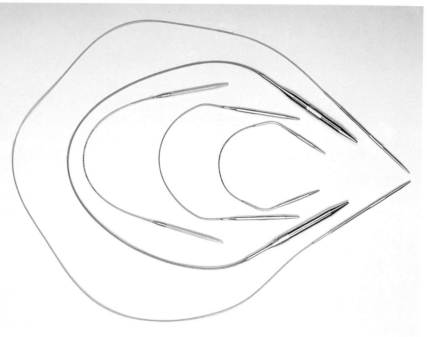

DOUBLE POINTED NEEDLES

Double pointed needles are generally used when working small projects in the round, such as socks, mittens, or gloves. When using double pointed needles, the stitches are divided evenly over three, or sometimes four, needles, and the remaining needle is used to work the stitches. The resulting seamless garment is the same as that produced by the circular needle, but a set of double pointed needles allows you to easily maneuver around the knitted piece within a tighter radius. Double pointed needles usually come in sets of 4 or 5 needles and in lengths of 7 or 10 inches.

Straight vs. Circular Needles

While straight needles are more basic and less expensive than circular needles, circular needles do offer some advantages that make them worth considering. The main benefit of using a circular needle over a pair of straight needles is basically one of comfort: knitting in a small space (such as on an airplane or in a car) is much easier with circular needles than with straight needles, which protrude outward from the knitting. Circular needles also allow the bulk of the stitches to slide around onto the plastic tubing that connects the two needles. This allows you to rest the work in your lap while knitting the stitches remaining on the needles rather than having to hold all of the stitches up on the right needle as you complete those on the left. Before you purchase needles for your first project, think about where you will be knitting and how important comfort is to you. It might just be worth spending the few extra dollars to purchase the circular needles.

Other Equipment

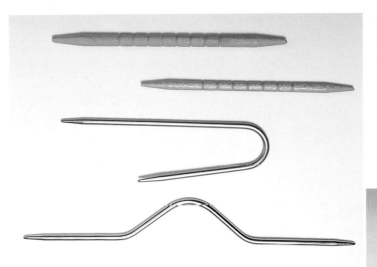

CABLE NEEDLES
Used to hold stitches when working cables (see pages 97–98).

TAPESTRY NEEDLES
Used in finishing to sew up seams and run in ends (see pages 57–60). They come in both straight and bent-tipped varieties.

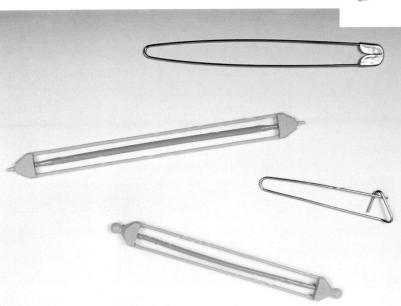

TAPE MEASURE
Used to measure knitted pieces or people to check for the fit of a garment. Can also be used to check gauge.

STITCH HOLDERS
Used to temporarily hold a group of stitches while continuing to knit others (see "Working the Thumb" on page 94 for an example).

CROCHET HOOKS

Used to correct mistakes by rescuing dropped stitches (see pages 45–46) or to create trims and accents in finishing (see page 112).

POINT PROTECTORS

Used to cap the tip of the needle to prevent stitches from slipping off the ends when not knitting. Come in a variety of shapes and sizes.

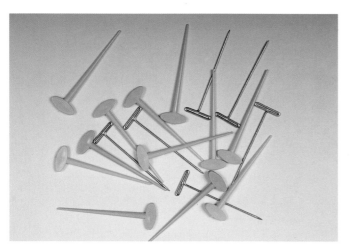

SEAMING PINS

Used to hold knitted pieces together when sewing seams or when blocking a large garment (see pages 56–57).

SMALL SCISSORS/ YARN CUTTER

Used to cut yarn. Pendant contains a recessed blade accessible through notches in its edges.

8

ROW MARKERS

Used to slip over needle to indicate start of a round of circular knitting (see pages 74–76). Split markers can be used to indicate placement of seams or stitches.

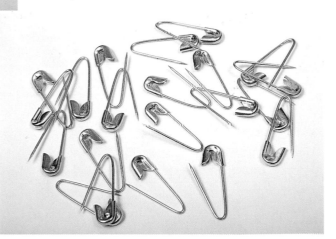

COILLESS PINS

Used like a split ring marker to indicate placement. Regular safety pins' coils get caught in yarn.

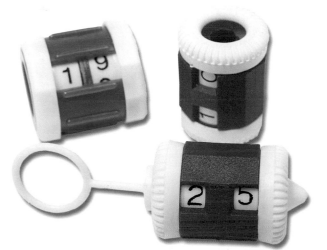

ROW COUNTERS

Used to keep track of rows as you knit. The round ones slip over a single-pointed needle for easy access. The pegboard keeps track of both rows and increases and decreases in more complicated patterns.

BOBBINS

Used to hold small portions of yarn when knitting individual rows with more than one color.

NEEDLE/STITCH GAUGE

Used to check gauge of knitted swatch (see pages 27–28) as well as to confirm size of unknown knitting needles.

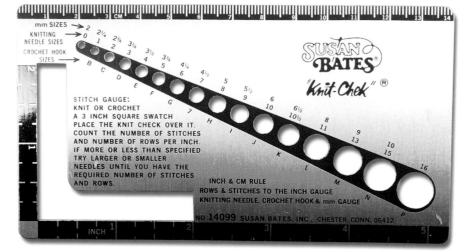

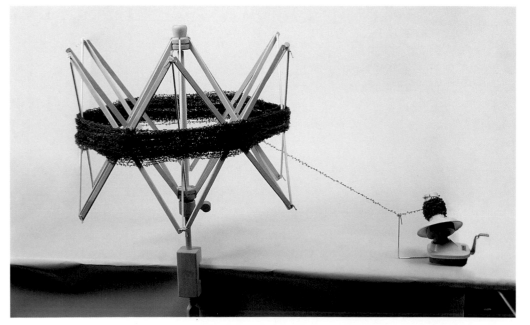

BALL WINDER/ YARN SWIFT

Used to wind hanks of yarn into easy-to-use balls. Both clamp onto the edge of a table or countertop.

Holding Yarn and Needles

At first it may feel awkward to hold the yarn and needles as shown, but over time that clumsy feeling diminishes as you gain more control. The initial goal of a beginning knitter is to hold the yarn and needles in such a way that it allows the knitter to obtain an even and consistent gauge (see pages 27–28 for more about gauge). To begin, use a shorter pair of needles in a medium size—a 6, 7, or 8 will work well. The first step in knitting is to make a slip knot (see pages 13–14 for instructions). Then, cast on a row of stitches (see pages 15–16 for instructions). Now you're able to explore the two methods of holding yarn and needles: the English Method and the Continental Method. Work through the general explanations of each method to see which you prefer.

Hold the needles loosely, like this.

Left-Handed Knitters

Unlike many crafts, knitting is primarily an ambidextrous activity. Other than using the tapestry needle to bind off or sew up seams and the scissors to snip the yarn, the left-handed knitter should be able to learn how to knit in exactly the same manner as the right-handed knitter. It may be easier, however, for lefties to learn using the Continental method.

English vs. Continental Knitting Methods

Although the majority of knitters in North America and Great Britain knit by holding the working yarn in their right hands (known as the English method), in Germany, France, and most other European countries, knitters hold the working yarn in their left hand (known as the Continental method). English-style knitters "throw" the yarn over the needle, while Continental-style knitters "pick" the yarn through the loop. Both methods produce the same basic end product, so the choice of method is a personal one that depends mainly on how you were first taught to knit. Some knitters prefer the Continental style, as it is faster and more efficient than the English style. The best advice for beginners who have not yet developed a preference is to try both methods and stick with whichever one feels most comfortable. If you do choose to knit Continental-style, however, it is essential to form the stitches exactly as described on pages 22–23 and 25 in order to avoid twisting them.

English-style knitting

Continental-style knitting

ENGLISH METHOD

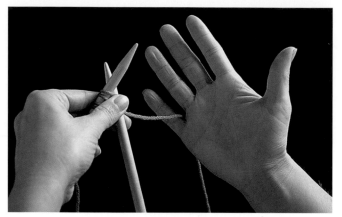

1. Hold both needles in your left hand by crossing the right needle tip under the left needle tip and grasping both between your thumb and middle finger. Drape the yarn attached to the ball (referred to as the working yarn) over your little finger.

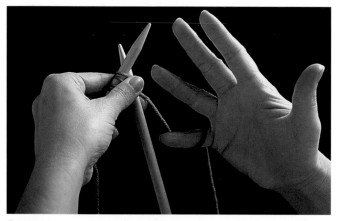

2. Wrap the yarn counterclockwise around your little finger for tension.

3. Insert your index finger under the working yarn between your little finger and the needle. You will use your index finger to carry the yarn around the tip of the right needle. With the index finger still holding the yarn, pass the right needle (on the bottom) into your right hand.

CONTINENTAL METHOD

1. Hold the needle with the cast on stitches in your right hand, with the working yarn draped over the little finger of your left hand.

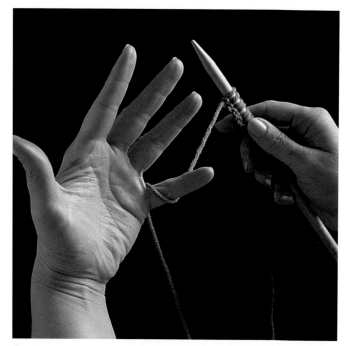

2. Wrap the yarn counterclockwise around your finger for tension.

3. Wrap the yarn over the index finger of your left hand, leaving about 2 inches of yarn between your index finger and the needle.

4. Return the needle with the cast on stitches to your left hand, supporting the needle with your thumb and middle and ring fingers.

Note: Throughout this book, the majority of examples are illustrated by an English-style knitter. In most cases, knitting method has no impact on the technique involved in forming a stitch. Where there are significant differences between the two methods (as in the yarn over increase on pages 63–65), both methods will be shown.

Making a Slip Knot

The first step in beginning to knit is creating a slip knot.

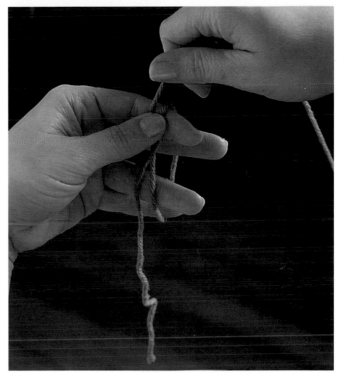

1. Holding the palm of your left hand toward you, drape 8 inches of yarn over the four fingers of your left hand, leaving a 5-inch tail. Wrap the yarn around the back of your fingers and back around to the front, stopping at your index finger. Hold the end of the yarn down with your thumb.

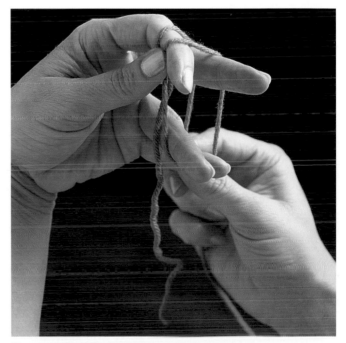

2. Continue the wrap around the back of your hand, stopping when you reach your little finger.

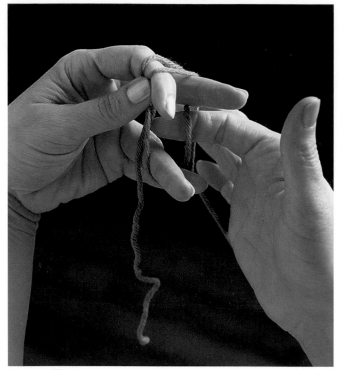

3. Spread your index and middle fingers slightly, and pull the working yarn up and through the loop.

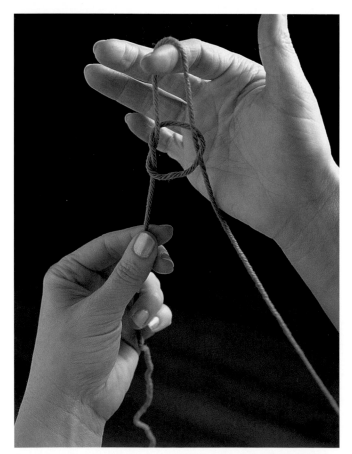

4. Once the working yarn is through, gently pull the loop off your fingers while holding onto the tail end of the yarn to form the knot.

5. Slide the loop onto the needle and pull the working yarn to tighten the loop on the needle.

A finished slip knot on the needle

14

Casting On

Casting on creates the stitches with which you will begin to knit. There are two basic methods of casting on, the cable and the long-tail.

THE CABLE CAST ON
This simple, versatile cast on is best suited for knitted pieces with non-elastic edges, such as scarves and afghans, that do not include ribbing.

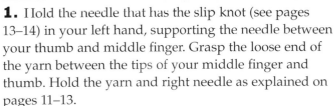

1. Hold the needle that has the slip knot (see pages 13–14) in your left hand, supporting the needle between your thumb and middle finger. Grasp the loose end of the yarn between the tips of your middle finger and thumb. Hold the yarn and right needle as explained on pages 11–13.

3. Holding the working yarn in your right hand, wrap the yarn counterclockwise (around) the tip of the right needle.

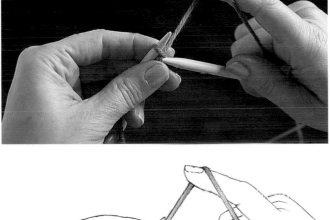

2. Insert the tip of the right needle into the loop beneath the left needle from right to left.

Tip: If you properly support the left needle between your middle finger and thumb, your index finger will be free to help manipulate the yarn.

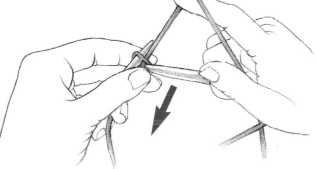

4. Using your right index finger (or left index finger for Continental knitters) for tension, pull the yarn down and through the loop with the tip of the right needle.

A newly created loop on your right needle

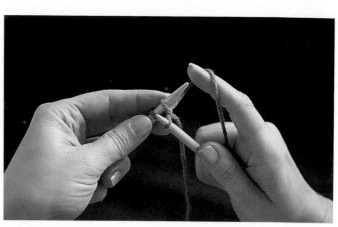

Repeating Step 4

5. Transfer the new loop on your right needle back onto your left needle and pull the working yarn gently to tighten.

6. Repeat Steps 2–5, using the newly made loop on the left needle each time, until you have cast on the required number of stitches.

Repeating Step 5

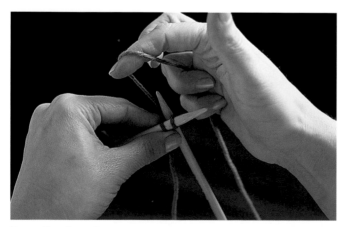

Repeating Step 2

A full row of cast on stitches

Tip: Don't pull your cast-on stitches too tight on the needle. They should be loose enough that the needle slips comfortably beneath each new loop.

THE LONG-TAIL CAST ON

For garments such as sweaters, socks, or hats that require a more elastic edge, the long-tail cast on is a better choice than the cable method. In this method, you estimate how much yarn will be required for the cast on stitches, leaving enough yarn for an adequate tail.

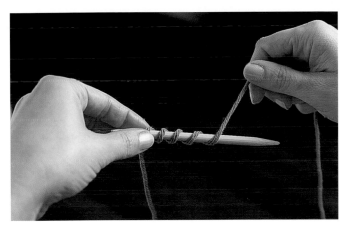

1. Estimate how much yarn you need for your tail by simply wrapping the yarn around the needle: one wrap for each stitch to be cast on. Add an additional 3-inch length of yarn to run in later.

2. Unwrap the loops and use that length as the tail. Make a slip knot as explained on pages 13–14.

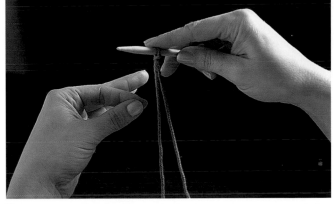

3. Holding the needle with the loop on it in your right hand, let the working yarn and tail hang straight down from the needle, with the working yarn behind the tail. Hold the thumb and index finger of your left hand together.

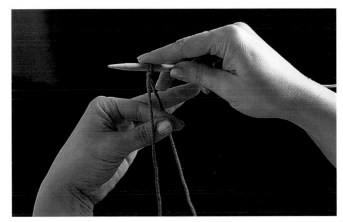

4. Insert your thumb and index finger in between the two dangling pieces or yarn.

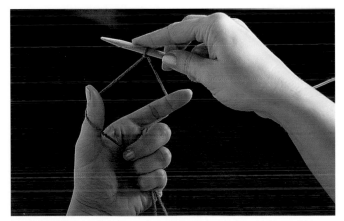

5. Pull the needle toward you, wrapping the working yarn clockwise around your left index finger and the tail counterclockwise around your thumb. (This process looks a lot like making a slingshot.)

6. Draw both ends into your palm and hold them down with your remaining fingers. The needle in your right hand and your left hand with the yarn should be straight up and down, with a little slack between the two.

7. Push the needle up through the loop on your thumb from the bottom.

8. Catch the working yarn on your index finger and draw it down through the loop.

The Long-Tail Cast On

If you think of the pieces of yarn on your fingers as individual strands, numbered from front to back, you will pass the needle under 1 and over 2, over 3, and then pull 3 back through 1 and 2. (You never touch 4.)

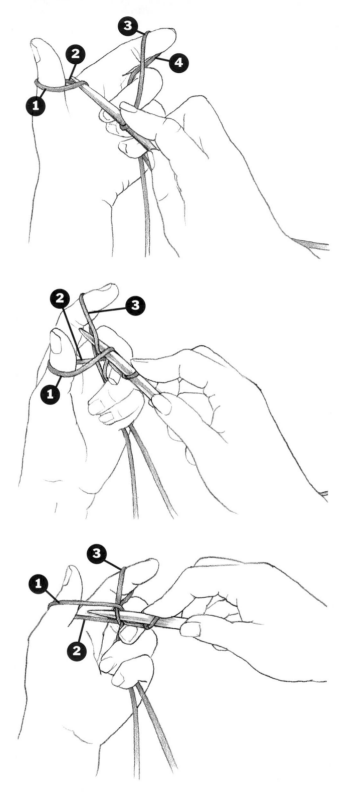

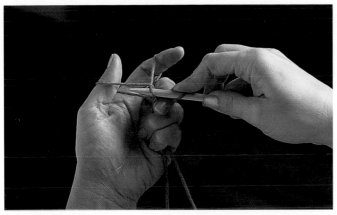

9. Pull the working yarn through the loop.

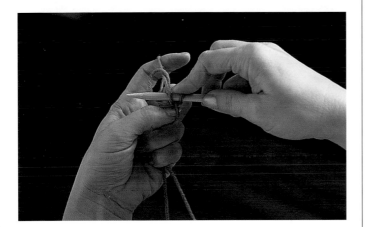

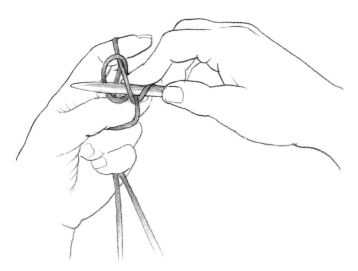

10. Release the loop of yarn from your thumb, gently pulling down on the tail with your thumb to tighten the loop.

11. Continue pulling down with your thumb until the loop is snug on the needle.

12. Reposition the yarn on your thumb and index finger and repeat Steps 6–11 until you have the required number of stitches.

Repeating Step 6

Repeating Step 10

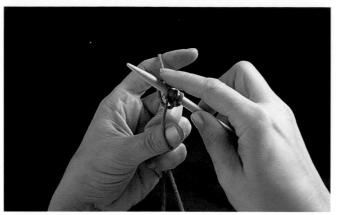

Repeating Step 11

Tip: Don't let go of the yarn in your palm. Make sure when you re-wrap the yarn around your thumb that you wrap counter-clockwise.

Stitches cast on by the long-tail method

Tip: This method produces a cast on that is smooth on the front and bumpy on the back. Because of this, it is necessary that you make the first row of your knitting a wrong-side row (for example, if you are knitting in stockinette stitch, start with a purl row rather than a knit row).

Knit

There are two basic stitches used in knitting: knit and purl. Both the English and Continental methods of knitting are shown here. To learn how to knit, first cast on 20 stitches using the cable method discussed on pages 15–16.

KNIT STITCH: ENGLISH METHOD

1. Hold the needle with the cast on stitches in your left hand. Push the top stitch down about 1 inch away from the tip of the needle.

2. Wrap the working yarn around your right index finger and hold it with the empty right needle in your right hand (as shown on page 12). Insert the tip of the right needle into the first stitch on the left needle from front to back, under the left needle.

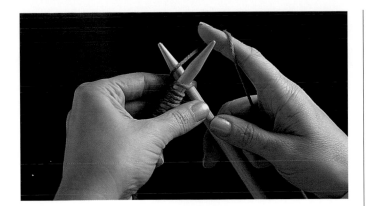

Yarn pulled through stitch

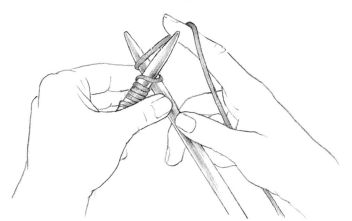

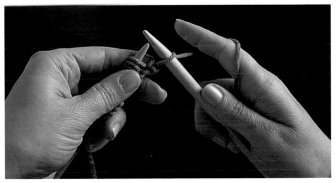

3. Using your right index finger, pass the yarn counterclockwise around the right needle and hold it there, parallel to the first stitch. Keep the tension comfortably tight with your right index finger.

5. Slip the first stitch off the left needle, leaving the newly knit stitch on the right one. You have just knit one stitch.

6. Repeat Steps 2–5 to knit through all the stitches on the left needle. You should always have a total of 20 stitches between the two needles. As you progress through the row, keep sliding the stitches on the right needle down to keep them from bunching up. Keep your knitting loose enough that the stitches slide easily along the needle.

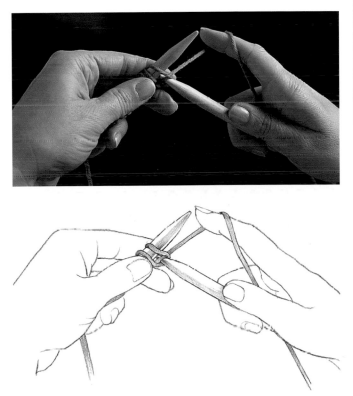

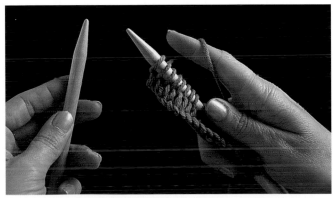

4. Use the tip of the right needle to pull the yarn down and through the stitch on the left needle.

7. When you have transferred all the stitches on your left needle to the right, you have completed one row of knitting. Turn the work around, making the old right needle the new left one, and vice versa, and knit a few more rows for practice. Knitting every row forms a pattern known as garter stitch, the most basic pattern. The resulting swatch will look the same on both sides.

KNIT STITCH: CONTINENTAL METHOD

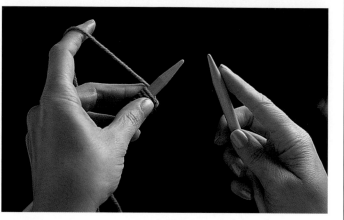

1. Wrap the working yarn around your left hand and hold it with the needle with the cast on stitches as shown on pages 12–13. Push the top stitch down about 1 inch away from the tip of the needle.

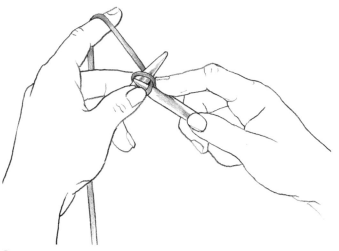

3. Catch the working yarn by putting the tip of the right needle on top of and behind it. Use your middle finger to help guide the yarn over the tip of the right needle. Pull the yarn through the stitch on the left needle.

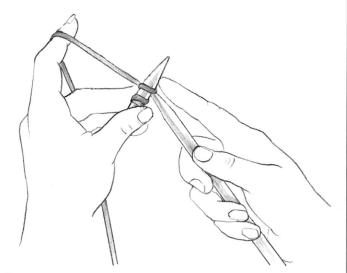

2. Insert the empty right needle into the first stitch on the left needle from front to back, under the left needle.

4. Slip the first stitch off the left needle, leaving the newly knit stitch on the right one. You have just knit one stitch.

5. Repeat Steps 2–4 to knit through all the stitches on the left needle. You should always have a total of 20 stitches between the two needles. As you progress through the row, keep sliding the stitches on the right needle down to keep them from bunching up. Keep your knitting loose enough that the stitches slide easily along the needle.

6. When you have transferred all the stitches on your left needle to the right, you have completed one row of knitting. Turn the work around, making the old right needle the new left one, and vice versa, and knit a few more rows for practice. Knitting every row forms a pattern known as garter stitch, the most basic pattern. The resulting swatch will look the same on both sides.

Purl

The purl stitch is the opposite of the knit stitch. Both the English and Continental methods of purling are shown here. To learn how to purl, first cast on 20 stitches using the cable method discussed on pages 15–16.

PURL STITCH: ENGLISH METHOD

1. Hold the needle with the stitches in your left hand. Push the top stitch down about 1 inch away from the tip of the needle.

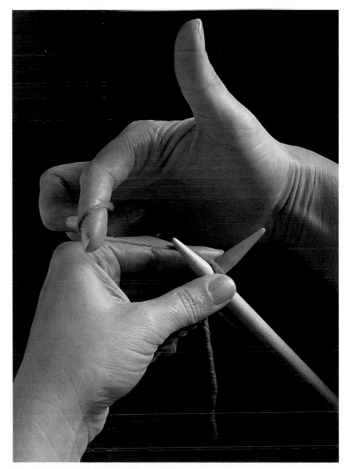

2. Holding the working yarn in front of the needle, insert the tip of the right needle into the first stitch on the left needle from back to front, in front of the left needle. Hold both needles between the thumb and index finger of your left hand.

3. Using your right index finger, pass the yarn counter-clockwise around the right needle.

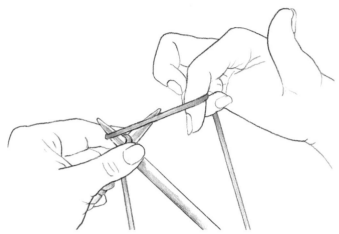

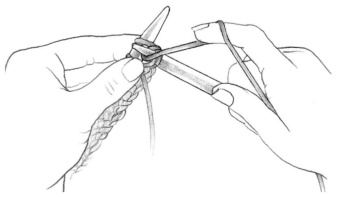

4. Use the tip of the right needle to pull the yarn back and through the stitch on the left needle.

5. Continue pulling the yarn completely through the stitch.

6. Slip the first stitch off the left needle, leaving the newly purled stitch on the right one. You have just purled one stitch.

7. Repeat Steps 2–6 to purl through all the stitches on the left needle. You should always have a total of 20 stitches between the two needles. As you progress through the row, keep sliding the stitches on the right needle down to keep them from bunching up. Keep your knitting loose enough that the stitches slide easily along the needle.

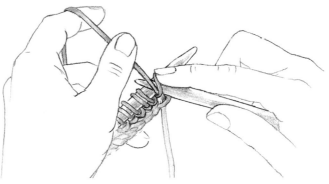

8. When you have transferred all the stitches on your left needle to the right, you have completed one row of purling. Turn the work around, making the old right needle the new left one, and vice versa, and purl a few more rows for practice.

Tip: When doing the first purl stitch of the row, it is important to insert the right needle into the stitch on the left needle before wrapping the yarn around your finger. This ensures that the yarn is in the right position before beginning your stitch. This only applies to the first stitch in the row; in subsequent stitches the yarn is already in the correct position.

3. Using your left thumb to guide it, place the yarn over the tip of the right needle from front to back, parallel to the stitch on the left needle.

PURL STITCH: CONTINENTAL METHOD

1. Wrap the working yarn around your left hand and hold it with the needle containing the cast on stitches as shown on pages 12–13. Push the top stitch down about 1 inch away from the tip of the needle.

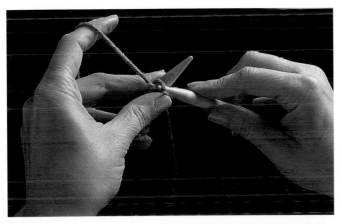

2. Holding the working yarn in front of the left needle, insert the empty right needle into the first stitch on the left needle from back to front, in front of the left needle.

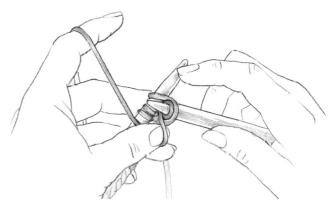

4. Using your thumb to keep tension on the working yarn, pull the loop up and through the stitch on the left needle.

5. Pull the loop the rest of the way through the first stitch and slip it off the left needle, leaving the newly purled stitch on the right one. You have just purled one stitch.

6. Repeat Steps 2–5 to purl through all the stitches on the left needle. You should always have a total of 20 stitches between the two needles. As you progress through the row, keep sliding the stitches on the right needle down to keep them from bunching up. Keep your knitting loose enough that the stitches slide easily along the needle.

7. When you have transferred all the stitches on your left needle to the right, you have completed one row of purling. Turn the work around, making the old right needle the new left one, and vice versa, and purl a few more rows for practice.

Stockinette Stitch

Now that you have mastered the two fundamental stitches of knitting, you will combine them into knitting's most basic pattern: stockinette stitch. In stockinette stitch, you simply alternate rows of knit stitches with rows of purl stitches. The result is a knitted piece with a smooth right side and a bumpy wrong side.

Try a practice swatch in stockinette stitch:

1. Cast on 20 stitches by the cable method, as described on pages 15–16.

2. Knit across the first row of stitches, as explained on pages 20–23.

3. Purl across the second row of stitches, as explained on pages 23–26.

4. Alternate knit and purl rows to create a swatch.

The right side of a stockinette swatch

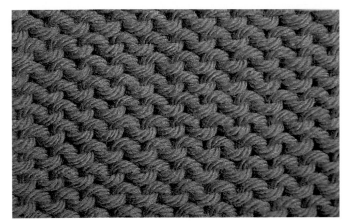

The wrong side of a stockinette swatch

Tip: Try to keep your stitches consistent in tension. Some beginning knitters purl more loosely than they knit. Controlling the tension with your index finger as you pull the yarn through the stitch is important. You will gain better control of this as you become more experienced.

Gauge

Gauge is without a doubt the single most important consideration when undertaking a knitting project. Unfortunately, however, in their eagerness to begin a new project, many knitters pay only a fleeting bit of attention to gauge or, worse yet, ignore it all together.

Every knitting pattern provides you with a gauge, a fixed number of stitches and rows per inch that are required to ensure that the piece or garment will fit properly. Depending on how loose or tight you knit, you may need to make adjustments in order to match this gauge.

1. Knit a 4 x 4 inch square sample swatch with the needles and yarn you plan to use for the garment. Work the swatch in the pattern specified for the garment (garter stitch, stockinette stitch, seed stitch, etc.). If no pattern is specified, work the swatch in stockinette stitch (knit one row, purl one row). Make sure to cast on at least four more stitches than you need to make a 4-inch swatch, since edge stitches are an unreliable measure of gauge. Bind off.

2. Measure your gauge on the swatch by laying the piece flat on a smooth, hard surface such as a table. Lay a gauge check along the edge of the piece. Count the number of stitches that fall within the 2-inch range. Each "V" in stockinette stitch represents a stitch.

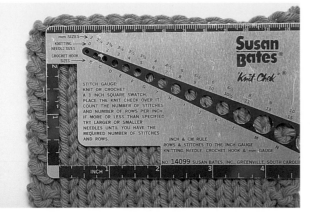

3. Lay the gauge check vertically across the center of the swatch and count the number of rows. Each "V" in stockinette stitch represents a row.

Compare your number of stitches and rows to the gauge stated on your pattern. If you have exactly the right number of stitches and rows, then you are ready to start your project. If not, then you need to make a few adjustments:

- If your swatch has too many stitches or rows, your knitting is tighter than it should be, and you need to increase the size of your needles to obtain the correct gauge.
- If your swatch has too few stitches or rows, your knitting is looser than it should be, and you need to decrease the size of your needles to obtain the correct gauge.

Repeat Steps 1–3 with either larger or smaller needles. Go up or down by a single size: for example, if your swatch had too many stitches when knit on a size 6 needle, try again on a size 7.

Tip: The type of yarn you use has a great deal to do with the gauge. If you are unable to find the exact yarn specified in the pattern, then you will need to try to find a substitute yarn as close in weight and fiber content as possible. Most yarns include a gauge on the ball band; try to come as close as possible to matching the original yarn's gauge.

Shaping: Increases and Decreases

You could keep knitting on your practice swatch indefinitely, continuing to knit and purl on the same 20 stitches that you cast on. Eventually, you would produce a long, narrow piece, appropriate perhaps for a thin scarf or belt. But in knitting other garments such as sweaters and vests, it is necessary to change the shape of the garment; to either add or subtract stitches in order to make armholes, collars, or cuffs. You can also use increases and decreases for decorative purposes (see the Bay Side Scarf on page 61). There are various methods of increasing and decreasing the number of stitches in a garment. The main ones are covered below.

Increases

BAR INCREASE
The simplest and most common increase method is called the bar increase. This increase is preferable in shaping, as it leaves no hole in the finished garment.

1. On a knit row, knit to the point in the row where you want to work the increase.

2. Knit the next stitch as usual, but do not slip it off the left needle.

3. With the stitch still on the left needle, insert the right needle into the stitch again, but this time from the back of the loop.

Make sure to insert the needle into the BACK of the loop.

4. Knit the stitch as usual, then slip both stitches off the left needle. The second stitch should have a small loop of yarn at its base, the "bar" of the increase's name.

A bar increase on a knit side row. Note the horizontal bar at the base of the increased stitch.

To work a bar increase on a purl side row:

1. On a purl row of your knitted swatch, purl to the point in the row that you want to work the increase.

2. Purl the next stitch, but do not slip it off the left needle.

3. With the stitch still on the left needle, insert the right needle up through the stitch again, but this time from the back of the loop.

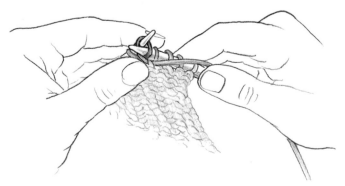

Make sure to insert the needle into the BACK of the loop.

4. Purl the stitch as usual, then slip both stitches off the left needle.

When working a bar increase on a purl side row, you will see the "bar" only on the right side of the knitted piece.

RAISED INCREASE

The raised increase is useful when adding stitches in the body or sleeves of a garment. Like the bar increase, it shows no hole and—even better—it is practically invisible in the finished garment.

1. On a knit row of your swatch, knit to the point in the row that you want to work the increase. Before you knit the next stitch, tilt your needles toward you so you can see the back of the knitting. Locate the stitch directly below the next stitch on your left needle.

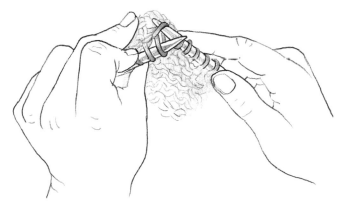

2. Insert the tip of your right needle into the back of the loop of this stitch.

3. Tilt the knitting back to normal position with the stitch on the right needle.

4. Knit through the stitch but do not slip it off the needle.

5. Knit the stitch on the left needle and slip it off the needle.

A raised increase on a knit side row

To work a raised increase on a purl row:

1. On a purl row of your swatch, purl to the point in the row that you want to work the increase. Now locate the stitch directly below the next stitch on your left needle. (It's the "bump" at the base of the stitch.)

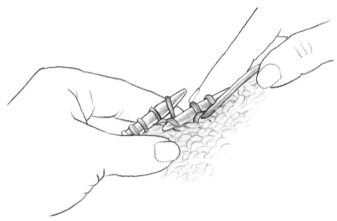

2. Insert the tip of your right needle into this stitch.

3. Bring the stitch into position and prepare to purl it.

4. Purl through the stitch but do not slip it off the needle.

5. Purl the stitch on the left needle and slip it off the needle.

A raised increase on a purl side row

MAKE ONE (M1)

This increase is commonly used in shaping garments. In this method, the increase is worked into the "ladder" between the two stitches from the previous row of knitting. Two different versions of the increase, the right slant and left slant, are typically used in conjunction with one another to provide a symmetrical increase.

Make One (Left Slant)

1. On a knit row of your swatch, knit to the point in the row that you want to work the increase. Before knitting the next stitch, gently spread the needles apart. Notice the strand of yarn that bridges the gap between these two stitches.

2. Insert the tip of the left needle (not the right needle) from front to back under this "ladder" and lift it onto the left needle.

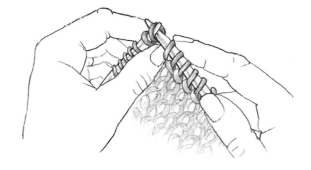

3. Insert the tip of the right needle through the back of the stitch.

4. Knit the stitch.

5. Slide the new stitch off the needle and knit the rest of the row as usual.

An M1 (left slant) increase on a knit side row

To work this increase on a purl row:

1. Purl to the point in the row that you want to work the increase. Before purling the next stitch, gently spread the needles apart. Notice the strand of yarn that bridges the gap between these two stitches.

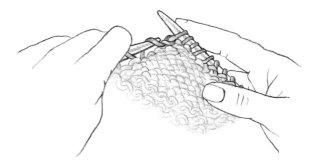

2. Insert the tip of the left needle from front to back under this "ladder" and lift it onto the left needle.

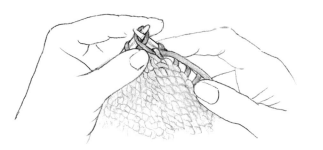

3. Insert the tip of the right needle through the back of the stitch.

4. Purl the stitch.

5. Slide the new stitch off the needle and purl the rest of the row as usual.

An M1 (left slant) increase on a purl side row as seen from the right side of the piece

Make One (Right Slant)

1. On a knit row of your swatch, knit to the point in the row that you want to work the increase. Before knitting the next stitch, gently spread the needles apart. Notice the strand of yarn that bridges the gap between these two stitches.

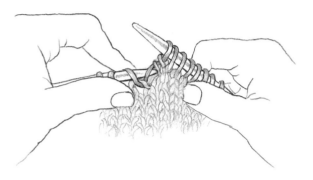

2. Insert the tip of the left needle (not the right needle) from back to front under this "ladder" and lift it onto the left needle.

3. Insert the tip of the right needle through the front of the stitch.

4. Knit the stitch.

5. Slide the new stitch off the needle and knit the rest of the row as usual.

An M1 (right slant) increase on a knit side row

36

To work this increase on a purl row:

1. Purl to the point in the row that you want to work the increase. Before purling the next stitch, gently spread the needles apart. Notice the strand of yarn that bridges the gap between these two stitches.

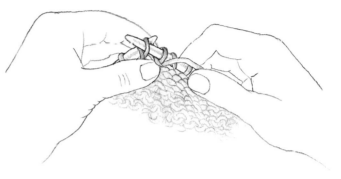

3. Insert the tip of the right needle through the front of the stitch.

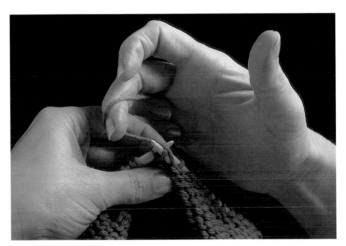

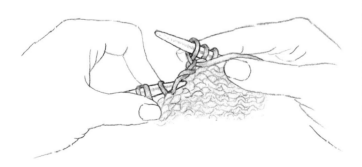

4. Purl the stitch.

2. Insert the tip of the left needle from back to front under this "ladder" and lift it onto the left needle.

5. Slide the new stitch off the needle and purl the rest of the row as usual.

An M1 (right slant) increase on a purl side row as seen from the right side of the piece

Note: A fourth increase method, the yarn over, is used for decorative purposes. See the Skill Workshop on pages 63–65 to learn how to work a yarn over.

Decreases

KNIT 2 TOGETHER (K2TOG)

This right-slanting decrease is usually used in conjunction with its mirror image, the left-slanting knit 2 together through back loops decrease (k2togtbl—see page 41). A common use is in shaping a sock (see page 79 for an example of these two decreases used for sock shaping).

1. On a knit row of your swatch, knit to the point in the row that you want to work the decrease.

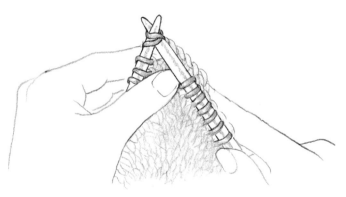

2. Insert the right needle into the next two stitches at the same time, as to knit.

Needle inserted into both stitches as to knit

3. Knit the two stitches together.

4. Slide the stitch onto the right needle and knit the rest of the row as usual.

A k2tog decrease on a knit side row

PURL 2 TOGETHER (P2TOG)

To create a right-slanting decrease from a purl side row, you can work a purl 2 together decrease (p2tog):

1. On a purl row of your swatch, purl to the point in the row that you want to work the decrease.

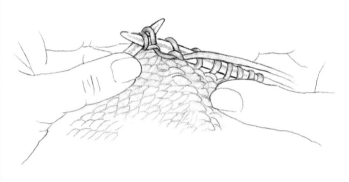

2. Insert the right needle into the next two stitches at the same time, as to purl.

Needle inserted into both stitches as to purl

3. Purl the two stitches together.

4. Slide the stitch off the needle and purl the rest of the row as usual.

A p2tog decrease from a purl side row

PURL 2 TOGETHER THROUGH BACK LOOPS (P2TOGTBL)

Another purl-side decrease is the purl 2 together through back loops (p2togtbl), which creates a left-slanting decrease on the knit side.

1. On a purl row, purl to the point in the row that you want to work the decrease.

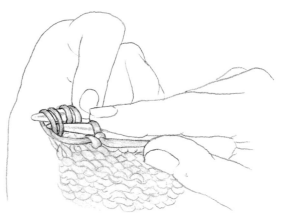

2. Bring the working yarn to the front, then turn the work toward you and push the right needle from right to left through the back of the loops.

Needle inserted through back of both loops

3. Purl the two stitches together through the backs of the stitches.

4. Slide the stitch off the needle and purl the rest of the row as usual.

A p2togtbl decrease from a purl side row

SLIP, SLIP, KNIT (SSK)

This is a subtle, left-slanting decrease.

1. On a knit row of your swatch, knit to the point in the row that you want to work the decrease.

2. Slip the next two stitches in the row by inserting the tip of your right needle into them as if to knit, but instead slide them onto the right needle without knitting them.

Both stitches slipped as if to knit

3. Insert the tip of the left needle into the front of the two slipped stitches to hold them in place.

Note: The k2togtbl decrease is frequently substituted for the ssk. The k2togtbl is worked like the k2tog decrease (see page 38), except that you will insert the needle into the back of the loops of the two stitches. It achieves the same result as the ssk—both slant to the left.

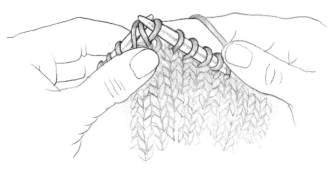

4. Knit the stitches together through the backs with the right needle.

5. Slide the two stitches off the left needle and knit the rest of the row as usual.

An ssk decrease from a knit side row

SLIP KNIT PASS (SKP)

This is a less-than-subtle left-slanting decrease and is usually used only in lace patterns or textured stitches.

1. On a knit row of your swatch, knit to the point in the row that you want to work the decrease.

2. Slip the next stitch by inserting the tip of your right needle into it as if to knit, but instead slide it onto the right needle without knitting it.

3. Knit the next stitch of the row as usual.

4. Insert the tip of the left needle into the slipped stitch and lift it up.

5. Pass the slipped stitch over the knit stitch and slide it off the right needle. Try not to stretch the stitch if possible.

6. Knit the rest of the row as usual.

An skp decrease from a knit side row

SLIP PURL PASS (SPP)

This purl side decrease causes a right-slanting decrease on the knit side of the piece. It is worked very similarly to the slip knit pass above.

1. On a purl row, purl to the point in the row that you want to work the decrease.

2. Slip the next stitch by inserting the tip of your right needle into it as if to purl, but instead slide it onto the right needle without purling it.

3. Purl the next stitch of the row as usual.

4. Insert the tip of the left needle into the slipped stitch and lift it up.

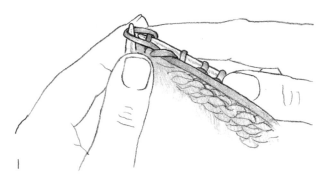

5. Pass the slipped stitch over the purl stitch and slide it off the right needle. Try not to stretch the stitch if possible.

6. Purl the rest of the row as usual.

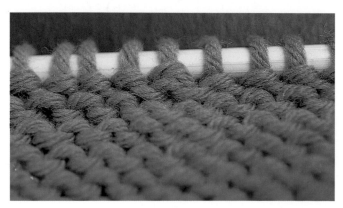

An spp decrease from a purl side row

Joining New Yarn

Whether you are knitting in one color or many, eventually you will run out of yarn and need to join a new ball. There are several different methods used to achieve this, but the simplest and most reliable is to secure the new yarn to the working yarn you have already been using by tying a knot.

1. At the beginning of a new row, cut the working yarn you have been using, making sure to leave at least a 3-inch tail. Have the yarn you want to join ready.

2. Make a loop in the new yarn and slide it over the needle. Leave at least a 3-inch tail to work in later.

3. Pull the loop of new yarn through the first stitch.

4. Continue to knit with the new yarn, being careful not to pull the tail through the first stitch.

5. After you've knit through four or five stitches in the row, turn the work to the back and fasten the two yarns with a square knot.

6. Pull the ends to secure the knot, then continue knitting the row as usual.

Picking Up Dropped Stitches

Even experienced knitters sometimes make mistakes. For beginners, the most common problem is "dropping" stitches. A dropped stitch is when a stitch accidentally slips off the needle and it unravels through the rows beneath it. Although this may look disastrous when you first spot it, it is in fact a fairly easy mistake to fix. You will need a crochet hook, slightly smaller than the thickness of the knitting needle you are using.

Tip: To minimize the problems caused by dropped stitches, recount the number of stitches on your needle frequently to make sure that you have not lost any stitches.

1. With the right side of the work toward you, visually trace the path of the dropped stitch down through the rows, noting the "ladders" it's created on the way.

2. Insert the crochet hook from front to back into the dropped stitch.

45

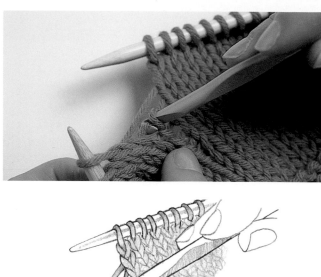

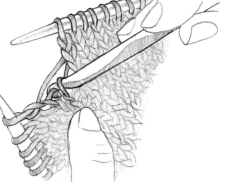

3. Pull the first ladder through the loop of the stitch.

4. Continue pulling the ladder through the stitch.

5. Remove the new stitch from the hook and hold it between your thumb and index finger.

6. Insert the crochet hook into this new stitch as in Step 2.

7. Continue working your way up through the rows in this manner, pulling the ladders through the loop of the stitch until you reach the top.

8. Replace the loop onto the needle, making sure not to twist the stitch when you do so.

A completed repair job

Tip: To repair a dropped stitch on a purl row, simply turn the work to the knit side and correct it as described above.

Taking Out Stitches

There will be times when, despite your most concentrated efforts, you will make a mistake in a pattern: you will forget to increase in a row or make a mistake that will throw off all the rows that follow. The best thing to do is to inspect your work often, counting your stitches and making sure that your pattern looks the way it should.

If you do find a mistake in a row that you have just completed, you can simply "unknit" the stitches in that row:

1. Identify the point in the row where the mistake was made (in this case, an errant purl stitch in a knit row, four stitches back).

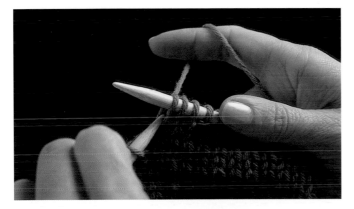

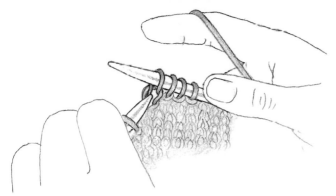

2. Insert the tip of the left needle into the stitch below the incorrect one.

3. Ease the working yarn out of the stitch and pull the right needle out.

4. Return the "unknit" stitch to the left needle.

5. Repeat Steps 2–4 until you reach the mistake.

Repeat Step 2

47

Repeat Step 3

Repeat Step 4

6. Correct the stitch(es) and continue with the row.

If you miss a mistake and continue to knit through subsequent rows, however, it is best to remove the stitches and reknit the rows. This is called unraveling or, more commonly, "ripping."

1. Locate your mistake and note how many rows you need to remove to reach it (in this case, two purl stitches in the middle of the previous row).

2. Lay the piece flat and slip the stitches off the needle by pulling the needle out from left to right.

3. Gently pull the working yarn to unravel the stitches.

4. Stop when you reach one row above the point of your mistake.

5. Pull out the stitches in the last row one by one using the technique explained on pages 47–48.

6. When you reach the point where the mistake appears, remove these stitches and correct them. Continue with the row according to the pattern.

Twisted Stitches

When placed on the needle correctly, a knit or purl stitch will form an upside-down U on the needle. The right side of the U will be to the front of the needle and the left side will be to the back. If a stitch is placed on the needle improperly, it is considered to be twisted, and must be fixed in order to ensure a clean, tight knitted piece. To fix a twisted stitch, simply remove it from the left needle with the point of the right needle (or vice versa) and replace it on the needle in the correct position. It is sometimes difficult for beginners to spot twisted stitches, but as you gain experience you will be able to see them right away.

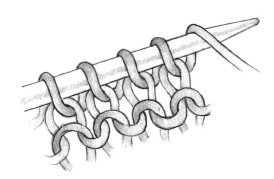

A row of correct knit stitches

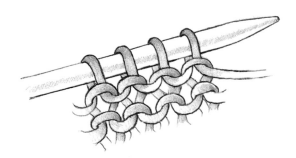

A row of correct purl stitches

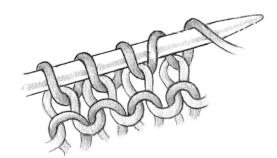

A twisted knit stitch

Binding Off

When you have completed your piece of knitting, you must secure the last row of stitches so they will not un-ravel. Binding off also secures stitches that are no longer required for a garment, such as at armholes or neck-lines.

Tip: It is common for beginning knitters to bind off too tightly, causing unsightly puckers along the edge of the garment. One way to avoid this is to bind off with a needle one or two sizes larger than the one you used to knit the rest of the piece.

1. On a knit row, knit the first two stitches of the row as usual.

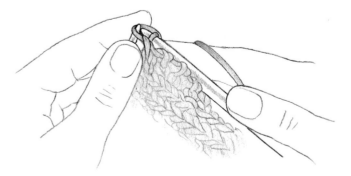

2. Using the point of the left needle, lift the first knit stitch up and pass it over the second stitch.

3. Slide the stitch off the right needle.

4. Knit the next stitch and repeat Steps 2–3 to bind off the rest of the row.

5. Continue binding off until you are left with only one stitch on your right needle.

6. Cut the working yarn, leaving a 3-inch tail.

A completed bound-off edge

To bind off on a purl side row, repeat as Steps 1–5 above, substituting a purl stitch for a knit stitch.

Tip: When binding off in ribbing or in any other pattern, adhere to the pattern when binding off the stitches: knit the knit stitches and purl the purl stitches.

The last stitch and tail

7. Pull the cut end through the final stitch to finish off. (You will learn what to do with this tail on page 60.)

Knitting from a Pattern

For the beginning knitter, knitting patterns can often appear confusing. But once you know the basic information the pattern communicates and what to do with it, they make much more sense. Take a look at the Biscayne Bay Shell pattern on pages 66–67. Each section is identified and explained below.

> **Tip:** Make sure you read the entire sentence in the pattern before starting to knit. Sometimes patterns contain more than one instruction per sentence.

GAUGE

As discussed, gauge is crucial to proper garment fit. In this case, the gauge is expressed as 20 stitches and 24 rows = 4 inches on a size 7 needle. Follow the steps on pages 26–27 to knit a test swatch and test your gauge before beginning this project.

MEASUREMENTS

Most garment patterns provide a range of sizes. You will first need to obtain accurate measurements for yourself or the intended wearer and then consult the pattern's sizing chart to determine which size is most appropriate. You will then cast on the correct number of stitches required to create that size of garment. You can also refer to the body measurement tables on pages 114–17 if the pattern does not include a sizing chart.

> **Tip:** One good way to get measurements for a knitted piece is to take a similar garment (your favorite sweater, for example) and lay it on a flat surface for measurement. Remember that the actual size of sweaters and other similar garments is measured across the widest part of the garment; length is measured from the top of the shoulder to the lower edge of the garment; and sleeve length is measured through the center of the sleeve from the shoulder seam to the cuff. Once you have the measurements of your favorite sweater, you can check them against the "actual" measurements in the pattern to see which size most closely corresponds with your ideal fit.

Once you've decided which size garment you want to knit, you will be able to determine how much yarn you will need and how many stitches you will initially need to cast on. Patterns usually use brackets to indicate additional sizes. The main size is listed first and subsequent larger sizes are listed in brackets following it: 32 [34, 36, 38]. When reading the pattern, you need to read only the number that corresponds in sequence to the size you are knitting. In other words, a pattern will say: "Cast on 64 [68, 72, 76] stitches." If you are knitting a size 36 garment, then you need to follow the second number within the brackets, or 72 stitches. Increases and decreases are also indicated in this manner, as are various other instructions such as repeating rows: "Repeat these two rows 6 [6, 8, 8] more times." It may be easier for you to read the pattern if you use a colored highlighter to indicate which numbers correspond to which size in the pattern. (If you knit the pattern again in a different size, choose a different color of highlighter.)

MATERIALS

This part of the pattern indicates which type of yarn is required for the project. Some patterns will specify brand names of yarns while others will indicate only the type of yarn (fingering, sport, worsted) that is needed. If you are knitting a one-size garment such as a throw, a set quantity of yarn will be specified. If the pattern is for several sizes, the quantity will depend on the size you plan to knit. This section will also list any other needles and equipment, such as stitch holders, zippers, or buttons, that are needed to complete the project.

> **Tip:** Make sure to purchase all the yarn you will need to complete your project at one time. Since yarn is usually dyed in batches, purchasing it at different times may result in having two skeins from different dye lots. The color can vary noticeably from dye lot to dye lot.

ABBREVIATIONS

Knitting patterns use abbreviations to save space when writing out instructions. Although they may seem a bit confusing at first, the more you knit the more they will become familiar. See page 113 for a list of the most common knitting abbreviations.

Asterisks (*) are often used in patterns to indicate instructions that need to be repeated. An asterisk will mark the beginning of a portion of the sequence that should be worked more than once. For example, "*k1, p1, k1, p5; rep from * to end" means that, after you've completed the sequence once, you repeat it again and again until you reach the end of the row. Parentheses are also used for a similar purpose. For example, "(k1, p1) twice" means k1, p1, k1, p1.

Part II

Projects

1

Teddy Bear Sweater

Gauge: 20 sts and 24 rows = 4"

Finished Chest Measurement: 12"

Materials:

       100% worsted weight wool

          Color A (MC): 100 yds

          Color B (CC): 100 yds

       US 7 Needles (or size to obtain gauge)

       Crochet Hook (size E)

NOTE: See page 121 for information on how to
obtain yarn for these projects.

This first project will allow you to put some of the basic skills you
learned in Part I of this book into practice in creating actual knitted garments. In the Teddy Bear Sweater, you will practice knitting
ribbing; working increases; as well as knitting in garter stitch, stockinette stitch, and reverse stockinette stitch. You will also learn the finishing techniques required to complete the other projects throughout
the book such as blocking, sewing up seams, and running in ends. It
is recommended that you complete this project first before moving
on to the other projects throughout the book.

BACK AND FRONT

Tip: Don't even think about starting to knit this little project without first knitting a 4-inch gauge swatch! See pages 27–28 for instructions on how to check and, if necessary, adjust to fit the required gauge.

CO 29 sts. Work 4 rows 1 x 1 rib inc'ing 2 st across last row (ws) 31 sts.

Work 4 rows gar st. Work 4 rows st st. Work 4 rows rev st st. Work 2 rows st st.

Using CC, *k1, sl1* rep from * to last st, k1. Purl 1 row.

Tip: gar st = garter stitch = knit every row
St st = stockinette stitch = knit 1 row on RS, purl 1 row on WS
Rev st st = reverse stockinette stitch = purl 1 row on RS, knit 1 row on WS

Armhole decrease row: k1, k2togtbl, k to last 3 sts, k2tog, k1. Purl 1 row. Rep last 2 rows 6x.

Tip: An ssk can be substituted for the k2togtbl—see page 41.

Using MC, *k1, sl1; rep from * to last st, k1. Purl 1 row (17 sts). Work 4 rows 1 x 1 rib. BO loosely in rib.

SLEEVES (KNIT 2)
Using MC, CO 19 sts. Work 4 rows 1 x 1 rib. Work 4 rows gar st. Work 4 rows st st.

Dec row: k1, k2togtbl, k to last 3 sts, k2tog, k1. Purl 1 row. Rep last 2 rows until 5 sts remain. Work 2 rows st st. Work 4 rows 1 x 1 rib. BO loosely in rib.

TIPS

- Since you know you'll be sewing up seams at the end of the project, make sure to leave a longer tail than usual when you cast on for the back and front.
- To create "1 x 1 rib," you will k1, p1 across the right side rows (Rows 1, 3, 5, etc.) and p1, k1 across the wrong side rows (Rows 2, 4, 6, etc.). It is very easy to lose track of how many rows you have completed, so be sure to use a row counter or pencil and paper.
- You should spread the two increases evenly across the last row (Row 4) by working one before the 10th stitch of the row and one before the 20th stitch. You also need to work the increases within the pattern, so make sure that you remember to knit the stitch after the increase. You can work the increase using any of the methods described on pages 28–38, but a make one, left slant increase paired with a make one, right slant increase creates a balanced row. Make sure to count your stitches at the end of the row to be sure you have 31.

FINISHING
Steam block pieces lightly. Sew sleeves to front and back as shown below. Sew up side seams on body and sleeves.

Assembling the Finished Pieces

I n the case of the Teddy Bear Sweater, the k1 before the decreases at the edges of both the front/back and the sleeves will provide this 1-stitch seam allowance. The seaming will pull the second stitch on both pieces together, pulling the seam allowance to the inside and forming a neat, invisible seam. Sew the bulk of the sleeve seam using the mattress stitch technique shown on pages 57–59. But when you reach the 1 x 1 rib at the top, work

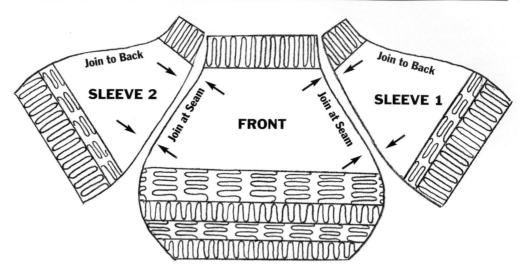

only a half-stitch seam allowance, catching the horizontal bars at the base of each stitch and pulling the two halves of the knit stitch from either side of the seam together to form a whole knit stitch in the rib pattern. Sew the side seams on the front/back and the arms in the same fashion.

SKILL WORKSHOP: FINISHING

T he term "finishing" is used to describe the various final steps you must take to complete your garment or knitted piece and make it ready to wear or display. No matter how well you complete the actual knitting, your garment will not look professional unless you pay careful attention to these finishing techniques. While you will no doubt be eager to finish your garment, fight the urge to rush through the finishing steps. The professional appearance of a well-finished garment will make you glad that you did.

Blocking

Blocking helps to even out the gauge of a finished knitted piece by relaxing the fibers of the yarn. While the piece is moist and pliable, you can adjust its size and shape slightly to fit the measurements specified in the pattern.

Tip: Depending on the type of project, some knitters do very minimal blocking. In the cabled vest in the photographs, for example, only the very edges of the front should be blocked to avoid flattening the cables that stand out from the texture. Additionally, you should never block ribbing that you want to remain elastic.

STEAM BLOCKING

1. Lay the garment wrong-side-up on a clean, smooth, flat surface. A carpeted floor will do fine. Smaller pieces of knitting can be blocked on an ironing board. Use round-headed pins or T-pins to pin the garment to the surface on which it will be blocked. Measure the piece as you go to make sure that it will be blocked to fit the dimensions specified in the pattern.

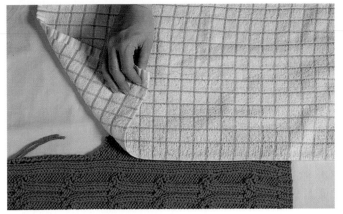

2. Place a clean press cloth over the section of the garment to be blocked.

3. Add water to your iron and set it on the steam setting. Hold the iron $1/2$ inch above the surface of the garment and allow the steam to flow over the cloth and onto the garment. Allow the garment to remain pinned to the surface until it dries.

WET BLOCKING

With this method, you simply pin the garment to the blocking surface and then use a fine-mist spray bottle to dampen the piece. Gently pat the surface of the garment to help the yarn fibers absorb the moisture. Adjust the shape or size of the garment as necessary, repin, and allow to lie flat until it is dry.

Seaming

In order to join together pieces of knitting into a finished garment, it is sometimes necessary to sew them together using a process known as seaming. It is best to seam pieces together using the tail of the yarn you left when you first cast on the piece to be joined. If you know that you will be seaming together a piece of knitting, make sure to leave a long enough tail to join it (a piece a little longer than the finished length of the edge should be adequate).

There are a number of different methods of seaming to choose from, but the most basic one, mattress stitch, will be shown here. This technique is worked one stitch in from the edge of the pieces to be joined together and is used on pieces that are knit in stockinette stitch.

Note: This method will work for all the seaming you will need to do for the projects in this book. See the Resources section on page 119 for details on books that teach more sophisticated finishing techniques.

1. Start by laying the two pieces to be joined right side up in front of you.

2. Thread the tail of the piece to be joined through a large tapestry needle.

Note: In the photos, a contrasting color of yarn is used to more effectively show the seam. In reality, the blue tail of the garment would be used to sew the seam.

3. Starting at the bottom of the piece without the tail (the piece on the left in the photo), insert the needle from wrong side to right side one stitch in from the corner.

5. On the other side of the seam (the piece without the tail), run the needle through the center of the first and second stitches, one row in from the edge.

4. Run the needle through the center of the first and second stitches of the first row of the piece with the tail, catching the two horizontal bars of yarn at the top of each stitch. Pull gently to tighten.

> **Tip:** If you fail to leave a tail long enough to sew the entire seam of your garment, start with a new piece of yarn, leaving a long enough tail to run in when you are finished sewing the seam.

6. Catch the two horizontal bars at the top of each stitch and pull gently to tighten.

7. On the side of the seam with the tail (the right piece), run the needle through the center of the first and second stitches, one row in from the edge. Catch the two horizontal bars at the top of each stitch and pull gently to tighten.

9. At the end of the seam, run in the remainder of the tail by weaving it through the stitches in the seam for at least 2 inches.

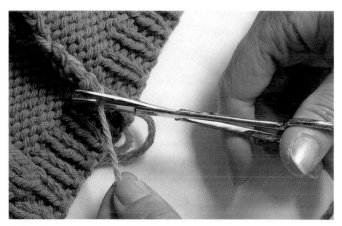

10. Cut the yarn close to the base of the last stitch.

8. Continue in this fashion up the length of the seam.

Running in Ends

Once you have sewn up all the seams in your garment, the final step in finishing it will be to turn it inside out and weave all the remaining loose tail ends into seams or through nearby stitches to make sure that they are secured snugly before cutting them. All your tails should be at least 3 inches long to begin with, so you should have no trouble threading these through a tapestry needle and running them in.

1. With the tail of the end threaded through a tapestry needle, weave it under at least 2 inches of purl stitch bumps.

2. Gently pull the needle all the way through the stitches, easing the yarn through as you go.

3. Pull snug to tighten, but don't pull so hard that the garment puckers.

4. Holding the garment flat, cut the end about $1/8$ of an inch from the last stitch the tail runs through.

5. Continue to run in the rest of the loose tail ends. Check to make sure that none of the ends show through on the right side of the garment.

Tip: When knitting with more than one color, try to run in the ends in a row of the same color as the tail end of the yarn.

2

Bay Side Scarf

Gauge: 28 sts and 32 rows to 4" on US 7 needles or size to obtain gauge

Materials:

Jaggerspun Zephyr (50% Merino Wool, 50% Tussah Silk)

Aegean Blue, 500 yds

Blueberry, 500 yds

US 7 Needles (or size to obtain gauge)

NOTE: Hold one strand of Aegean Blue and one strand of Blueberry together throughout scarf.

Approximate Measurements: 7.5" x 59"

This simple but lovely project will teach you a new method of increasing, the yarn over, which you will use to create the delicate lace pattern of the scarf. Since you won't need to worry about shaping or finishing, you will be free to enjoy creating the attractive lace pattern and savor the joy of knitting with the luxuriously soft silk/merino blend yarn.

SCARF

CO 55 sts loosely.

PATTERN

Rows 1–4 (Row 1 rs): Knit.

Rows 5, 7, 9, 11: k4, * [k2tog] 2x, [yo, k1] 3x, yo, [sl1, k1, psso] 2x, k1, rep from * to last 3 sts, k3.

Rows 6, 8, 10, 12: k3, purl to last 3 sts, k3.

These 12 rows form pattern.

Work in patt for 59" ending with Row 4. BO loosely.

Understanding the Pattern

On Rows 5, 7, 9, and 11 of the pattern:

1. k4: Knit the first 4 stitches of the row.

2. *[k2tog] 2x: Do two k2 decreases consecutively (see pages 38–39).

3. [yo, k1] 3x: Work the yarn over as described on the next page, followed by a knit stitch. Repeat this twice more.

4. yo, [sl1, k1, psso] 2x, k1: Work a single yarn over, then slip one stitch, knit one, and pass the slipped stitch over the knit stitch—this is the same as the slip knit pass on pages 42–43. Repeat the bracketed section again. Knit one stitch.

5. rep from * to last 3 sts, k3: Work the pattern from the asterisk (starting from Step 2 above) until 3 stitches remain on the left needle. Knit these last 3 stitches.

The delicate, lacy effect seen in this project is actually created by an increase method called a yarn over (yo). The yarn over increase creates a hole, or eyelet, in the piece by creating an extra stitch. In order to maintain the same number of stitches in the row, this increase is always balanced with a decrease elsewhere in the row. In these examples, the yo increase is immediately followed by a k2tog or a p2tog decrease in order to keep the number of stitches in the row constant.

English-Style Yarn Over between Two Knit Stitches

1. Knit the row up to the point where you will make the yarn over. Bring the yarn to the front and wrap it from front to back around the right needle.

2. Work a k2tog decrease immediately following the yo increase. Hold the yarn over in place on the right needle with your index finger as you work the decrease.

A yo increase paired with a k2tog decrease creates a "hole" in the knitting, which is often used in lace patterns.

Continental-Style Yarn Over between Two Knit Stitches

1. Knit to the point where you will make the yarn over. Pull the working yarn to the back and hold it in place with your index finger.

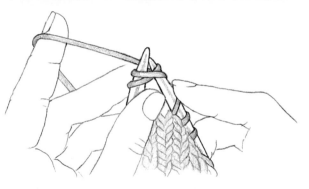

2. Continue holding down the yo with your index finger as you work the k2tog decrease.

The end result of a yo + k2tog decrease is the same, whether you use the Continental or English method.

English-Style Yarn Over between Two Purl Stitches

1. Purl the row up to the point where you will make the yarn over. Bring the yarn to the back over the top of the needle and then toward the front between the two needles.

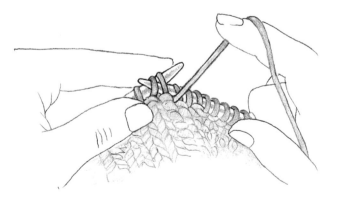

2. Work a p2tog decrease immediately following the yo increase. Hold the yarn over in place on the right needle with your index finger as you work the decrease.

A yo increase paired with a p2tog decrease

Tip: When doing a yarn over between a knit and a purl stitch, be sure to bring the yarn to the front between the needles after the knit stitch, then forward by carrying it over the top of the right needle and forward. If you fail to do this, it will not create an additional stitch. Similarly, when doing a yarn over between a purl and a knit stitch, make sure to bring the yarn to the back by carrying it over the top of the right needle.

Continental-Style Yarn Over between Two Purl Stitches

1. Purl the row up to the point where you will make the yarn over. Wrap the yarn from front to back around the right needle. Hold the yarn in place at the front of the work with your thumb.

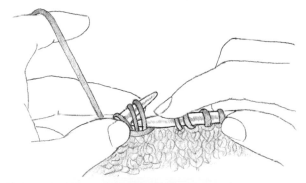

2. Continue holding down the yo with your thumb as you work the p2tog decrease.

A yo + p2tog decrease worked Continental style

3

Biscayne Bay Shell

Gauge: 18 sts and 26 rows to 4" in St st on US 7 needles or size to obtain gauge

Finished Measurements:

Bust 36 (38.5, 41, 44, 46.5)"
Length 20 (21, 22, 23, 24)"

Materials:

Wool in the Woods Terrain (80% Cotton, 20% Rayon, 200 yds/skein)

Color A: 1 (2, 2, 2, 2) skein(s)

Color B: 2 (3, 3, 4, 4) skeins

US 7 Needles (or size to obtain gauge)

5 Stitch Holders (2 6-inch, 3 4½-inch)

NOTE: When using hand dyed yarns, remember to vary skeins throughout to maintain color quality.

This attractive sleeveless shell is the perfect project on which to perfect your garment-knitting skills. The simple stockinette stitch pattern will allow you to focus your concentration on shaping and finishing. You will also learn how to pick up and knit stitches along an edge and how to sew shoulder seams together from stitches on a holder. You can work the front and back of this garment on either a straight or a circular needle (see the discussion of straight vs. circular needles on page 6 for more advice on making this decision), but it will be easier to knit back and forth on a circular needle when working the neck and armhole bindings.

Biscayne Bay Shell

BACK

With A, CO 81 (87, 93, 99, 105) sts. Knit 4 rows. Work St st beg on RS for 3". Knit 2 rows. With B, knit 2 rows. Work in St st until piece measures 11.5 (12, 13, 13.5, 14.5)".

ARMHOLE SHAPING

BO 4 sts each side 1x. BO 3 sts each side 1x. BO 2 sts each side 1x. Dec 1 st each side every other row 4x (4x, 5x, 5x, 5x). Dec 1 st each side every 4th row 2x, 51 (57, 61, 67, 73) sts. Work in St st until piece measures 19 (20, 21, 22, 23)".

Tip: You can only bind off at the beginning of the row. (See pages 50–51 for information on how to bind off.) You will have to knit 2 rows to bind off 4 stitches on each side 1 time, 2 more rows to bind off 3 stitches on each side 1 time, and then 2 more rows to bind off 2 stitches on each side 1 time. To make sure that your increases slant in the direction of the armhole shaping, do a k2togtbl or ssk decrease on the right side of the piece and a k2tog decrease on the left side.

NECK SHAPING (work both shoulders together)

Work 14 (16, 17, 19, 21) sts, place next 23 (25, 27, 29, 31) sts on a holder, add another ball of yarn, work remaining 14 (16, 17, 19, 21) sts. BO 2 each neck edge 1x, 12 (14, 15, 17, 19) sts. Work even until piece measures 20 (21, 22, 23, 24)". Place shoulder sts on a holder.

Tip: To add another ball of yarn, simply put down the first ball (do not cut the yarn) and start knitting the stitches after the holder with the new ball. Leave a 10- or 12-inch tail for seaming. Work only the 2 sets of 14 (16, 17, 29, 21) stitches on each side of the holder. Leave the 23 (25, 27, 29, 31) stitches on the holder alone. You will pick up these stitches later when you start the neck binding.

FRONT

Work as for back until piece measures 16.5 (17.5, 18, 19, 20)".

Tip: You will work the front to 11.5 (12, 13, 13.5, 14.5)" and then do the armhole shaping as above. Continue on these 51 (57, 61, 67, 73) stitches until the piece measures 16.5 (17.5, 18, 19, 20)" and then work the neck shaping below.

NECK SHAPING (work both fronts together)

Work 18 (20, 21, 23, 25) sts, place next 15 (17, 19, 21, 23) sts on a holder, add another ball of yarn, work remaining 18 (20, 21, 23, 25) sts. BO 2 each neck edge 2x. Dec 1 st each neck edge every other row, 2x, 12 (14, 15, 17, 19) sts. Work even until piece measures 20 (21, 22, 23, 24)".

FINISHING

Knit shoulder seams of front and back together.

Tip: See the Skill Workshop on pages 70–71 for details on how to knit the shoulder seams together.

NECK BINDING

With RS facing and Color A, pick up (pu) and k18 (18, 20, 20, 20) sts from shoulder to front holder, k15 (17, 19, 21, 23) sts from holder, pu and k18 (18, 20, 20, 20) sts from front holder to shoulder seam, pu and k5 sts to back holder, k23 (25, 27, 29, 31) sts from holder, pu and k5 sts to shoulder seam. PM. Purl 1 row. Knit 1 row. Purl 1 row. BO loosely in knit.

Tip: If you haven't already been using one, you will need to switch to a circular needle to work the neck and armhole bindings (you could also use a set of double pointed needles). You will pick up the 2 sets of 18 (18, 20, 20, 20) stitches along the front neck edges as well as the extra 10 stitches you will pick up on either side of the back holder (5 on each side). Be sure to space these stitches evenly. See pages 68–69 for details on how to pick up stitches.

ARMHOLE BINDINGS

With RS facing and Color A, pu and k92 (94, 94, 96, 96) sts around armhole opening. Knit 1 row. BO loosely in knit.

Sew side seams.

When joining pieces of a garment together, it is often possible to avoid sewing them together using a technique by which stitches are "picked up" from the edge of the piece that is to be joined. This technique eliminates the bulky seam that comes from joining a garment by sewing and is used most commonly on neckbands, armholes, or borders.

TIPS

- Although the pattern may state "pick up and knit," what it really means is "pick up as if to knit." Once you have the stitch on your needle, do not knit it again. You will knit or purl through the entire row once you have picked up all the stitches along the seam.
- If the seam to be joined is a longer one (a side seam, for example), first lay the piece on a flat surface and use pins or stitch markers to divide the edge to be joined into equal sections of 2–3 inches. Then determine how many stitches you need to pick up in each marked section by dividing the total number of stitches required by the number of sections. Spread this number of stitches evenly across the section. This will ensure that the stitches to be picked up are distributed evenly over the length of the edge.

To pick up stitches along the edge of a piece of knitting:

1. With the right side of the piece facing you, start at the right edge of the piece and insert the needle under the first stitch.

2. Make a loop with the new yarn and slip it over the needle.

3. Knit through this loop as you would a regular knit stitch.

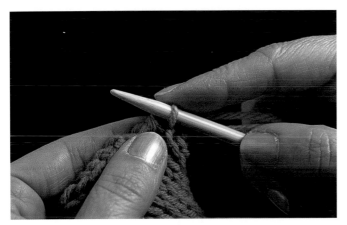

The new stitch on the right needle is the first picked up stitch.

4. Repeat Steps 2–3 along the length of the piece, picking up the evenly distributed number of stitches between each marker.

The second picked up stitch

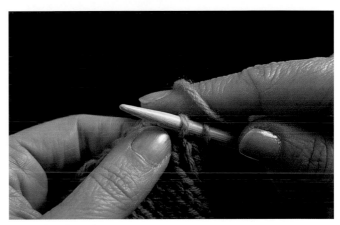

Repeating Step 3

A row of picked up stitches

Tip: After you pick up all the stitches across the edge on the right needle, you will be at the end of the right side of the garment (the far left edge). If you are knitting in a pattern, you will need to return to the right side of the garment to start the pattern by turning the work to the wrong side and purling a row. Once you turn the work back to the right side you can start working your pattern.

The 3-needle bind off provides the ideal way to join together two identical seams smoothly and evenly. This technique should be used to join the shoulder seams in both the Biscayne Bay Shell and the Seattle Bound Vest (page 94). When using this technique, the stitches should still be on the needles (or on a stitch holder) and each needle must have the same number of stitches as the other one.

To join the shoulder seams together using this technique:

1. Place the two right sides of the garment together, with the stitches to be joined still on the needles and the stitch holder. Hold the needle and the holder parallel.

Tip: Make sure to use a large stitch holder so you will have plenty of room to knit from it.

2. Insert a third needle into the first two stitches on both needles, as if to knit.

3. Knit the two stitches together. You should have one stitch on the right needle.

4. Repeat Step 2 with the next set of stitches, knitting them together as one. You will now have two stitches on the right needle.

5. Using the point of the left needle, lift the first knit stitch up and pass it over the second stitch.

6. Slide the stitch off the right needle.

7. Knit the next set of two stitches and repeat Steps 5–6 to bind off the next set of stitches on the right needle.

8. Continue binding off until you are left with only one stitch on your right needle.

9. Cut the working yarn, leaving a 3-inch tail, and pull the cut end through the final stitch to finish off.

The shoulder seam from the right side of the garment

4

Northwest Ridge Hat

Gauge: 21 sts and 26 rows to 4" in St st on US 6 needles or size to obtain gauge

Materials:

Cascade 220 (100% Pure New Wool, 100 g/3.5 oz/220 yds/skein)

1 skein of each:

Color A: 4008 (maroon)
Color B: 9338 (olive)
Color C: 4006 (rust)
Color D: 4011 (taupe)

Cascade does not give names for colors, only numbers. The color names in parentheses are for reference only.

16" Circular US 4 Needles (or size to obtain gauge)

16" Circular US 6 Needles (or size to obtain gauge)

Stitch Markers

NOTE: If you have chosen to knit the matching Northwest Ridge Mittens (see page 89), there will be ample yarn remaining for the hat.

This fun hat can be knit on its own or in conjunction with the matching Northwest Ridge Mittens on page 89. In this project you will learn how to knit in the round on a circular needle and gain experience with joining new balls of yarn from the frequent color changes in the pattern (see pages 44–45 for a refresher on this technique). The Skill Workshop will also teach you how to create the narrow tube of knitted cording that can be used, as it is here, as a drawstring or in numerous applications in other projects. If you have jumped ahead in the book and already completed the mittens, you will have more than enough yarn left over to complete the hat.

HAT

Using smaller needles and A, CO 120 sts. Pm and join. Work 1x1 rib for 2.75". Change to larger needles. With B, k14 rnds.

Dec rnd: * k2tog, k10; rep from * around. 110 sts.

PATTERN

Rnds 1, 5, 9: With A, * k5, p5; rep from * around.
Rnds 2, 6, 10: With A, * p5, k5; rep from * around.
Rnd 3: With B, work rnd 1.
Rnd 4: With B, work rnd 2.
Rnds 7 and 11: With C, work rnd 1.
Rnd 8: With C, work rnd 2.
With C, k13 rnds.
Dec rnd: * k2tog, k9; rep from * around. 100 sts.

PATTERN

Rnds 1, 5, 9: With A, * k5, p5; rep from * around.
Rnds 2, 6, 10: With A, * p5, k5; rep from * around.
Rnd 3: With C, work rnd 1.
Rnd 4: With C, work rnd 2.
Rnds 7 and 11: With D, work rnd 1.
Rnd 8: With D, work rnd 2.
With D, k6 rnds.
Eyelet Rnd: * k9, yo, k2tog; rep from * around. K6 rnds.

PATTERN

Rnds 1, 5: With A, * k5, p5; rep from * around.
Rnds 2, 6: With A, * p5, k5; rep from * around.
Rnd 3: With D, work rnd 1.
Rnd 4: With D, work rnd 2.
BO loosely in knit.

FINISHING

With smaller needle and C, co 3 sts. Work 3 st I-cord* for 16". BO. Weave I-cord through eyelet row and make overhand knot to close top of hat.

See the Skill Workshop on I-Cord on page 77.

TIPS

- To change to the larger needles, start knitting the stitches onto the larger needle at the beginning of the row where you need to make the change. This will save you from having to transfer the stitches one by one to the larger needle. Place one point protector at the empty end of the larger needle and one on the right end of the smaller needle to keep stitches from slipping off the ends.
- Remember that in circular knitting, the right side of the work is always facing you, so to knit 1 x 1 rib you will knit 1, purl 1 continuously (unlike in straight knitting, where you must alternate between k1, p1 and p1, k1 rows).

SKILL WORKSHOP: KNITTING IN THE ROUND ON CIRCULAR NEEDLES

Up until this point, all the knitting you have done has been on two straight needles. Knitting on straight needles produces a flat piece of knitting that can be seamed together with another flat piece to form a garment, such as the front and back pieces of a sweater. Knitting in the round, however, produces a seamless, tubular piece of knitting that is perfect for hats, socks, or sleeves. There are two methods of knitting in the round; one requires a circular needle, the other a set of double pointed needles. The Northwest Ridge Hat and the 2 x 2 Socks make use of both of these methods.

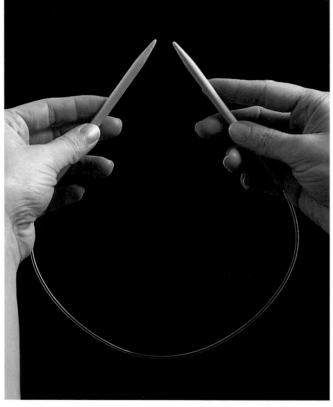

A circular needle

Circular needles are basically the tips of regular knitting needles joined by a thin, flexible strand of plastic. Stitches are knit on the tips of the needles in the usual fashion, then slid off the needles and onto the plastic as they are pushed around the circle. Circular needles come in various sizes and lengths: 12, 16, 20, 24, 32, and 40-inch lengths are available. Always use the length of needle that your pattern indicates. Knitting on a longer needle will stretch the stitches and distort the final piece.

1. Using a 16-inch circular needle, cast on the required number of stitches using the cable method in the same manner you cast on with straight needles. The stitches will slide around the bend of the circle. Take care not to pull or stretch them.

2. Insert a plastic marker over the tip of the right needle so you'll know where the round begins and ends.

3. Holding the circular needle with the first cast on stitch in your left hand, insert the needle into the first stitch.

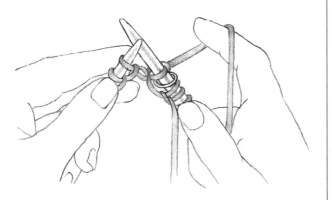

4. Knit into the first stitch, making sure the tension is high enough that the stitch is flush against the needle before sliding it off.

Twisted Stitches

Before you knit, it is essential to make sure that the stitches are not twisted on the needle. Lay the needle down on a flat surface and turn all stitches in so the cast on edge faces the center of the circle. If any stitches are twisted, correct them now. After you have knit the circle together, there is no way to fix twisted stitches other than removing them and starting again.

Properly positioned stitches

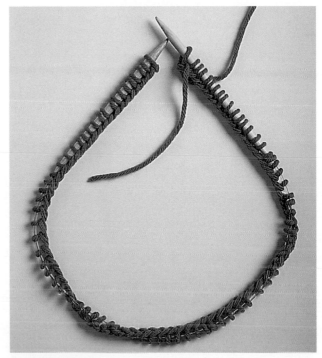

Twisted stitches

5. Continue knitting in this fashion, sliding the stitches around the needle as you go.

. . . to the tip of the right.

6. When you reach the end of the row . . .

One completed row of circular knitting

Tip: Unlike on straight needles, in which you turn the work from right to wrong side, when working on circular needles the right side of the knitting is always facing you. Because of this, in circular knitting, stockinette stitch is continuous knitting rather than alternating knit and purl rows.

. . . pass the marker from the tip of the left needle . . .

SKILL WORKSHOP: MAKING I-CORD

I-cord is a name first coined by knitting pioneer Elizabeth Zimmerman to describe easy-to-knit, decorative cording that has a multitude of uses in knitting projects. According to her daughter, Meg Swansen, the original technique was actually called "idiot cord," but Zimmermann "thought the name rather rude" and shortened it to "I-cord." See Elizabeth Zimmerman's classic book, *Knitting Workshop* (see the Resources section on page 119 for publication details), for many more creative applications for I-cord.

I-cord is incredibly easy to make:

1. Cast on 3, 4, 5, or even 6 stitches (depending on how wide you want your I-cord to be) using the cable method (see pages 15–16) on double pointed needles.

2. Knit across the first row but do not turn.

3. Slide the stitches to the opposite end of the needle.

4. Knit the next row as usual, from right to left. Pull the working yarn taut against the needle to avoid any gaps.

5. Repeat Steps 2–4 until your I-cord reaches the desired length.

2 x 2 Socks

Gauge: 26 sts and 36 rows to 4" in St st on US 3 needles or size to obtain gauge

Materials:

Wool in the Woods Twin Twist (92% Wool, 8% Nylon, 200 yds/skein), 2 skeins

US 3 Double Pointed Needles (or size to obtain gauge)

US 5 needles (any type)

Tapestry Needle

NOTE: When using hand dyed yarn, remember to vary skeins throughout to maintain color quality.

Some beginning knitters are needlessly intimidated by the idea of knitting socks. In reality, however, once you learn how to knit in the round on double pointed needles and master a few basic techniques, you can indulge yourself in the joy that is sock knitting. The Project in Progress section that accompanies this project will take you step-by-step through the two most complicated aspects of making a sock: turning the heel and creating the gusset. Nothing quite compares with the satisfaction of completing your first sock, and since they are fairly small, you can look forward to much quicker gratification.

LEG

CO 48 sts with larger needle. Divide sts onto 3 smaller double pointed needles with 16 sts on each needle. Work *k2, p2; rep from * around until leg measures 2". Work *p2, k2; rep from * around until leg measures 4". Work *k2, p2; rep from * around until leg measures 6".

HEEL

K12 (heel). Place next 24 sts on one needle. Place remaining 12 sts with first 12 heel sts. Row 1: (WS) sl1, purl to end of row. Row 2: sl1, knit to end of row. Repeat the last 2 rows until 22 total rows have been completed.

TO TURN HEEL

Row 1: (WS) p14, p2tog, p1, turn
Row 2: sl1, k5, k2togtbl, k1, turn
Row 3: sl1, p6, p2tog, p1, turn
Row 4: sl1, k7, k2togtbl, k1, turn
Row 5: sl1, p8, p2tog, p1, turn
Row 6: sl1, k9, k2togtbl, k1, turn
Row 7: sl1, p10, p2tog, turn
Row 8: sl1, k11, k2togtbl, k1, turn
Row 9: sl1, p12, p2tog, turn
Row 10: sl1, k12, k2togtbl

Tip: An ssk can be substituted for the k2togtbl—see page 41.

GUSSET

(RS) Pick up and k12 sts along right side of heel with extra needle. With another needle, k24 instep sts. With another needle, pick up and k12 sts up other side of heel. Continue to knit 7 sts from heel sts. Place remaining 7 sts on the first needle. Needles should contain 19, 24, 19 sts. Knit 1 rnd. Decrease next rnd as follows: Needle 1: k to last 3 sts, k2tog, k1; Needle 2: k24 sts;

Needle 3: k1, k2togtbl, k to end of rnd. Continue last row until 12 sts remain on Needles 1 and 3.

Tip: See the Project in Progress section on pages 85–88 for instructions on how to create and turn the heel and how to create the gusset.

FOOT

Work in rnds in St st until sock measures 3" from finished length.

TOE

Next (dec) rnd: Needle 1: k to last 3 sts, k2tog, k1; Needle 2: k1, k2togtbl, k to last 3 sts, k2tog, k1; Needle 3: k1, k2togtbl, k to end of rnd. K3 rnds. Work dec rnd, k3 rnds, work dec rnd. K2 rnds. Work dec rnd. K2 rnds. Work dec rnd. K1 rnd. Work dec rnd. K1 rnd. Work dec rnd, 2x. K 4 sts from Needle 1 to Needle 3. Weave 8 sts on one needle with 8 sts from other needle.

Tip: See the Skill Workshop on pages 82–84 for instructions on how to weave the last 16 toe stitches together.

Unlike their straight cousins, double pointed needles, as their name suggests, have points at both ends. Double pointed needles are generally called for when working smaller items such as socks, mittens, or gloves. The stitches are divided evenly over three, or sometimes four, needles and the remaining needle is used to work the stitches. Double pointed needles usually come in sets of four or five needles and in lengths of 7 or 10 inches.

It will feel awkward at first to manipulate this triangle (or square) of needles, but as with all awkwardness, it will diminish in time.

1. Cast on 24 stitches on two of the double pointed needles using either the cable or long-tail method (see pages 15–20).

2. Divide the stitches evenly among the three needles by sliding the first 8 stitches off the cast-on needle onto one of the double pointed needles.

3. Slide the next 8 stitches onto another needle. Start at the back of the needle (the end opposite the working yarn).

24 stitches divided among 3 double pointed needles

4. Hold the needles in a triangle shape, turning all the loops toward the inside of the triangle.

Tip: Position the stitches in the middle of each needle. Move them to the tip of the needle only as you are ready to knit them. This will prevent stitches from slipping off the ends of the needles.

5. Use the empty fourth needle to knit into the first cast-on stitch on the left needle (Needle 1).

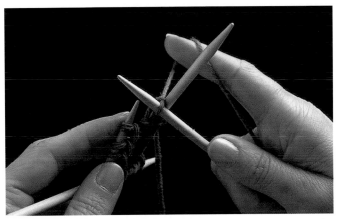

6. Slide the stitches off the left needle as you knit them. Don't be distracted by the dangling tail of yarn; trim it if it is longer than 3 inches and pull it down and out of the way of the working yarn.

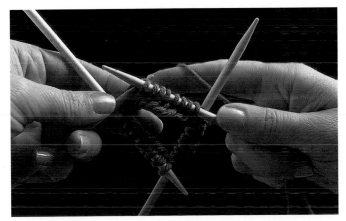

7. Knit the 8 stitches on the Needle 1, then rotate the triangle and start knitting into the first stitch on Needle 2. Try to pull the working yarn snug to the needle as you make the transition between the two needles in order to avoid gaps between them.

- Make sure that you recognize the difference between the knitting instructions for a needle and the instructions for a round. A round of knitting is made up of the knitting done on all three (or four) double pointed needles. Be sure to complete the required stitches for all of the needles before you move on to the next round.
- Make sure that the cast on stitches are not twisted on the needles. Turn all the loops so they face to the inside of the triangle. Be extremely careful that they do not twist—especially between the needles. At the end of your first round of knitting, go back and trace the loops of the stitches with your finger to ensure that none are twisted. If they are, you will need to remove the stitches and start again.
- As with knitting on a circular needle (see pages 74–76), when knitting on double pointed needles, the right side of the work is always facing you. This means that stockinette stitch is created by continuous knitting rather than alternating knit and purl rows.

8. Proceed to knit the 8 stitches on Needle 3. When you finish knitting these stitches and reach the marker, you have completed one round of knitting.

2 x 2 Socks

The most common method of knitting socks is from top to bottom, meaning that the last piece of the sock you knit is the toe. The best way to join together the stitches at the end of the toe into a smooth, tight seam is to use a grafting method called Kitchener stitch. The technique is named after Lord Kitchener, who during World War I contributed a sock pattern with a grafted toe for women in the United States and Canada to knit for the soldiers in the trenches.

To graft your sock's toe using Kitchener stitch:

2. Cut the working yarn, leaving an ample tail (at least twice the length of the stitches on the needles). Thread the tail through the eye of a tapestry needle.

1. Following the decrease rows at the toe of the sock, the pattern will ask you to knit the remaining stitches on one needle onto another needle. After doing so, you should have the same number of stitches on each needle, which should now be held parallel, with the wrong sides of the knitting facing one another.

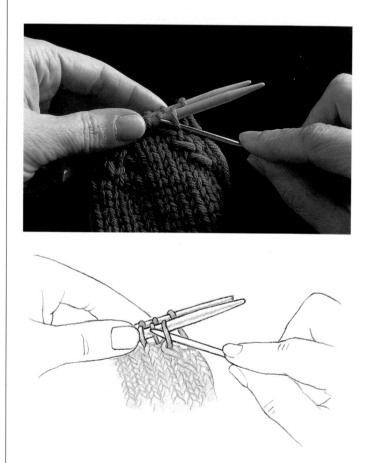

3. Holding the needles in your left hand, with the work pushed to the end of the points facing right, draw the tapestry needle through the first stitch on the front needle as if to purl. Leave it on the needle.

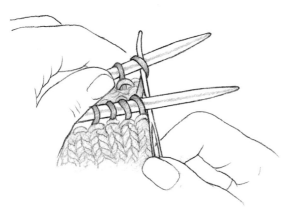

4. Now, draw the needle through the first stitch on the back needle as if to knit. Leave it on the needle.

Tip: The working yarn must pass under the needles when moving from front to back.

5. Draw the needle through the first stitch on the front needle as if to knit.

6. Slip the stitch off the needle.

Tip: Keep the tension constant throughout your grafting; try to match that of the sock itself. It is better to graft too loosely than too tightly. You can always go back and tighten loose grafting before you finish the seam.

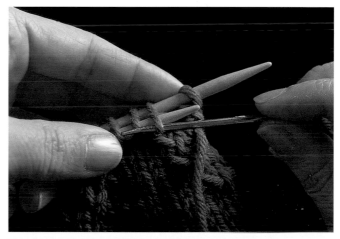

7. Draw the needle through the next stitch on the front needle as if to purl. Leave it on the needle.

8. Carrying the working yarn under the needles, draw the needle through the first stitch on the back needle as if to purl.

9. Slip the stitch off the needle.

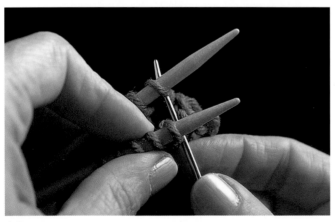

10. Draw the needle through the next stitch on the back needle as if to knit. Leave it on the needle.

11. Repeat Steps 5–10 until you have used up all the stitches on both needles and you have a complete seam.

12. Once your seam is complete, you will need to tighten it by gently pulling the working thread from the back end of the seam to the front. Use the needle to pull the loose seam stitches tighter. Don't pull too tightly.

A finished Kitchener stitch toe seam

2 x 2 Socks

84

Working the Heel

After your sock leg measures 6 inches in length, you are ready to start the heel. In order to create the heel, you will need to transfer the stitches from three double pointed needles onto two and then knit the heel straight (as opposed to in the round), knitting and purling back and forth across the 22 rows, slipping one stitch at the beginning of every row. You will pick up these slipped stitches later to form the basis of the foot of the sock.

1. Knit 12 stitches on Needle 1 and move the remaining 4 stitches onto Needle 2. Then place the first 4 stitches of Needle 3 with the 20 stitches now on Needle 2.

2. Place the remaining 12 stitches on Needle 3 with the 12 stitches you knit on Needle 1.

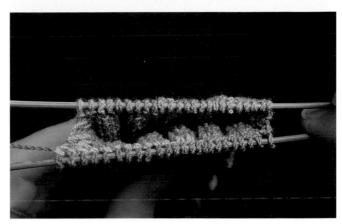

3. The front and back needle should each have 24 stitches.

4. Slip the first stitch of Row 1 (wrong side) as if to purl then purl across the rest of the row. Turn the work to the right side and slip the first stitch of Row 2 as if to knit and then knit across the remainder of the row. Continue in this fashion until 22 rows are completed. Use a stitch counter or pencil and paper to keep track of each row as you complete it.

The finished 22-row heel

Turning the Heel

Next you will need to "turn" the heel, by working a series of decreases across the next 10 rows. You will continue to knit and purl back and forth, slipping the first stitch of each row, and turn the work from wrong side to right side. This time, however, you will allow a few stitches to remain on the left needle and turn the work without completing them. This "short row," in combination with the decreases you'll make, will cause the heel to turn.

1. Starting with a wrong side row, purl 14 stitches across, purl 2 together, then purl 1. Now turn the work to the right side, leaving 7 stitches dangling to the side on the old left needle. Start Row 2 of the heel turn, remembering to slip the first stitch of the row.

Tip: Push these stitches to the middle of the needle so they do not slide off the needle.

2. When you complete Row 2, turn the work to the wrong side, again leaving 7 stitches on the side needle.

3. Work Row 3, slipping 1, purling 6. In order to complete the row, you will need to transfer 2 stitches from the side needle (containing the left-over 7 stitches from Row 1). Finish the row by purling 2 together and purling 1. Turn the work to the right side, leaving 5 stitches on the side needle.

4. Continue in this fashion until all 10 rows of the heel turn are completed. You will gradually use up the stitches on the side needles until on Rows 9 and 10, you will work straight across the row.

The finished turned heel

Creating the Gusset

In order to continue with the foot of the sock, you will need to pick up the stitches you slipped while working the heel. You will join these with the remaining 14 heel stitches (split over two needles) and then knit the 24 instep stitches on a third needle.

1. Using a spare needle (Needle 1), pick up 12 stitches along the right edge of the heel. It is fairly easy to pick out the slipped stitches: They lay on the top of the edge and should have a visible space underneath them. Visually identify these dropped stitches and plan which of them you intend to pick up. Make sure that you pick up the stitches closest to the intersection of the two needles; this will avoid holes around the corners of the gusset. You can also knit the stitch closest to the intersection through the back of the stitch to twist it (see page 29). This will help to cover holes.

Tip: See pages 68–69 for more details on picking up stitches.

2. Knit across the 24 instep stitches with another needle (Needle 2).

3. With another needle (Needle 3), pick up 12 stitches along the left edge of the heel, as in Step 1. With the same needle, continue to knit 7 stitches from the top heel stitches.

4. Place the remaining 7 stitches with the 12 picked up stitches on Needle 1. Needles 1 and 3 should now contain 19 stitches each, and Needle 2 should have 24.

5. Knit one round, then begin decrease rounds as indicated in the pattern.

6

Northwest Ridge Mittens

Gauge: 21 sts and 26 rows to 4" in St st on US 6 needles or size to obtain gauge

Materials:

Cascade 220 (100% Pure New Wool, 100 g/3.5 oz/220 yds/skein)

1 skein of each:

Color A: 4008 (maroon)
Color B: 9338 (olive)
Color C: 4006 (rust)
Color D: 4011 (taupe)

Cascade does not give names for colors, only numbers. The color names in parentheses are for reference only.

US 4 Double Pointed Needles

US 6 Double Pointed Needles (set of 5) (or size to obtain gauge)

1 3-inch Stitch Holder

NOTE: If you have chosen to knit the matching Northwest Ridge Hat (see page 72), there will be ample yarn remaining for mittens.

Intended to accompany the Northwest Ridge Hat (page 72), this project will build on the skill of knitting in the round on double pointed needles that you learned in Chapter 5. You will also use many of the same decrease techniques employed in shaping the toe of the sock as well as using Kitchener Stitch to weave the final stitches together. This project will also introduce a technique specific to mittens: creating and working the thumb. A Project in Progress section will explain this technique in step-by-step detail. If you have already worked the hat, you will have more than enough yarn left over to complete both mittens.

MITTEN

Using smaller needle and C, CO 42 sts. Divide sts onto 3 dpn with 14 sts on each needle. Join and work 1x1 rib for 2.25".

Change to larger needles. With B, k6 rnds.

Tip: When changing from one set of needles to another, simply start with one larger needle as the right needle and gradually knit the stitches off the smaller ones.

THUMB GUSSET FOR RIGHT MITTEN

Rnd 7: k2, inc in st just made, k1, inc in next st, k to end of rnd.

Rnds 8, 10, 12, 14, 16: Knit.

Rnd 9: k2, inc in st just made, k3, inc in next st, k to end of rnd.

Rnd 11: k2, inc in st just made, k5, inc in next st, k to end of rnd.

Rnd 13: k2, inc in st just made, k7, inc in next st, k to end of rnd.

Rnd 15: k2, inc in st just made, k9, inc in next st, k to end of rnd.

Tip: After the above increases, you should have 24 stitches on Needle 1. See the Project in Progress section on pages 91–92 for instructions on how to complete Round 17.

Rnd 17: k2, place next 11 sts on hold, turn work, CO 7 sts, turn work, k to end of rnd (48 sts).

Tip: Following Round 17 you should have 9 stitches on Needle 1 (7 of which were just cast on), 11 stitches on the holder, 11 stitches on Needle 2, 14 stitches on Needle 3, and 14 stitches on Needle 4.

THUMB GUSSET FOR LEFT MITTEN

Rnd 7: k19, inc in st just made, k1, inc in next st, k to end of rnd.

Rnds 8, 10, 12, 14, 16: Knit.

Rnd 9: k19, inc in st just made, k3, inc in next st, k to end of rnd.

Rnd 11: k19, inc in st just made, k5, inc in next st, k to end of rnd.

Rnd 13: k19, inc in st just made, k7, inc in next st, k to end of rnd.

Rnd 15: k19, inc in st just made, k9, inc in next st, k to end of rnd.

Tip: After the above increases, you should have 24 stitches on Needle 2. See the Project in Progress on pages 91–92 for instructions on how to complete Round 17.

Rnd 17: k19, place next 11 sts on hold, turn work, CO 7 sts, turn work, k to end of rnd (48 sts).

Tip: Following Round 17 you should have 14 stitches on Needle 1, 12 stitches on Needle 2 (7 of which were just cast on), 11 stitches on the holder, 8 stitches on Needle 3, and 14 stitches on Needle 4.

Knit 4 rnds. Work patt as follows:

PATTERN

Rnds 1, 5, 9: With A, * k4, p4; rep from * around.
Rnds 2, 6, 10: With A, * p4, k4; rep from * around.
Rnd 3: With B, work rnd 1.
Rnd 4: With B, work rnd 2.
Rnds 7 and 11: With D, work rnd 1.
Rnd 8: With D, work rnd 2.

With D, work rnd 1 of patt. K6 rnds. Divide sts onto 4 dpn with 12 sts on each needle.

Ded rnd: k2, k2togtbl, k to end of first needle; k to last 4 sts, k2tog, k2 on second needle; k2, k2togtbl, k to end of third needle; k to last 4 sts, k2tog, k2 on fourth needle. Knit 2 rnds. Work 1 dec rnd. Work 1 knit rnd. Rep last 2 rnds until 5 sts rem on each needle. K2togtbl 2x, k1, cont to second needle with same needle, k1, k2tog 2x, with another needle, k2togtbl 2x, k1, cont to fourth needle with same needle, k1, k2tog 2x. 6 sts will rem on each of 2 needles. Weave 6 sts from front needle to back needle.

Tip: An ssk can be substituted for the k2togtbl—see page 41.

THUMB

With spare needle and B, k11 sts from holder; with another spare needle pu and k7 sts across CO sts. Divide sts onto 3 dpn as follows: with spare needle k7, with another needle k6, with another needle k5, k1 from first needle onto third needle, 6 sts on each needle. Knit in rnds for desired length of thumb.

Tip: See page 93 in the Project in Progress for tips on how to work the thumb.

DECREASE ROUNDS

Rnd 1: k2togtbl, k4 on first needle; k1, k2tog, k2togtbl, k1 on second needle; k4, k2tog on third needle.
Rnd 2: k2togtbl, k3 on first needle; k2tog, k2togtbl, on second needle; k3, k2tog on third needle.
Rnd 3: k2togtbl, k1 on first needle, sl next st to second needle; k2tog, sl next st from third needle to second needle, k2togtbl; k1, k2tog on third needle.

Divide sts onto 2 needles as follows: Sl 1 st from second needle to first needle. Sl 1 st from second needle to third needle. Weave 3 sts from front needle to back needle.

Creating the Thumb Gusset

You will work a series of increases on Needle 1 (for the right mitten) or Needle 2 (for the left mitten) to create a gusset for the thumb of the mitten. Because of the increases, the gusset will puff up a little and stand up from the rest of the knitted fabric.

Once all the increases are complete, you will transfer the stitches that make up the gusset to a stitch holder. You will leave these stitches on the holder and knit them later to create the front of the mitten's thumb. You will also need to cast on additional stitches to knit the back of the thumb. You will leave these stitches as a selvedge edge and pick them up later when you are ready to knit the thumb.

The completed thumb gusset

1. Knit the first 2 stitches (right mitten)/19 stitches (left mitten), then place the next 11 stitches on a stitch holder.

11 thumb stitches on holder

2. Turn the work so the wrong side of the knitting is facing you. With the fifth double pointed needle, cast on 7 stitches, placing them on the left needle with the other 2 stitches (right mitten)/5 stitches (left mitten).

7 cast on stitches on needle plus other 2 stitches

3. Turn the work back so the right side is facing you. With the fifth double pointed needle, knit the 11 stitches (right mitten)/8 stitches (left mitten) after the holder. Make sure to pull the working yarn taut against the needle to avoid any gaps between the cast on stitches and the other stitches.

4. Knit to the end of the round as usual.

5. Knit 4 more rounds, as specified, then continue knitting in the pattern.

The thumb gusset after knitting 4 rounds

Working the Thumb

You will work the thumb last. After you've completed the mitten and woven the stitches together at the top, you will have free needles with which to finish knitting the thumb.

1. Using yarn B, knit the 11 stitches off the holder onto a double pointed needle. Leave a 6-inch tail of the yarn to work in later.

2. With another double pointed needle, pick up the 7 stitches across the back of the thumb (see pages 68–69 for tips on how to pick up stitches).

The back needle contains the 11 stitches knit off the holder and the front needle contains the 7 stitches picked up along the back of the thumb.

3. Divide the stitches among 3 double pointed needles by knitting 7 of the stitches that had been on the holder with Needle 1; then, with Needle 2, knit the next 4 stitches on that needle and continue to knit the first 2 stitches on the back of the thumb; then knit the remaining 5 stitches with Needle 3. Knit 1 stitch from Needle 1 onto Needle 3. You should have 6 stitches on each needle.

4. Continue to knit the thumb in the round until you reach the desired length, then work the decrease rounds and weave stitches together as indicated.

7

Seattle Bound Vest

Gauge: 16 sts and 20 rows to 4" on US 9 needles or size to obtain gauge

Finished Bust Measurement:
38.5" (43", 46", 49")

Finished Length:
20.5" (22", 24", 25")

Materials

Skacel Merino Light (100% Superwash Merino Wool, 75m/50g/82 yds/skein), 7 (9, 11, 13) balls; (color shown: #11)

US 9 Needles (or size to obtain gauge)

5 Stitch Holders (2 6-inch, 3 4½-inch)

This project will not only allow you to practice the garment-knitting skills you learned in Chapter 3, but it will also teach you a new technique, knitting cables, that can be applied to many different kinds of projects. As you will learn in the Skill Workshop, the basic cabling technique is actually quite simple; more intricate cable patterns are accomplished by varying the number of stitches cabled and increasing the frequency of the repeat of the cable. In the vest shown here, a relatively simple cable pattern is embedded within a 16-row pattern of stockinette and reverse stockinette stitch. The effect is dramatic.

SPECIAL ABBREVIATIONS

C4F: Slip next 2 stitches onto cable needle and hold at front of work, knit next 2 stitches, then transfer and knit 2 stitches from cable needle

C4B: Slip next 2 stitches onto cable needle and hold at back of work, knit next 2 stitches, then transfer and knit 2 stitches from cable needle

T2F: Slip next stitch onto cable needle and hold at front of work, purl next stitch, then transfer and knit stitch from cable needle

T2B: Slip next stitch onto cable needle and hold at back of work, knit next stitch, then transfer and purl stitch from cable needle

CABLE PATTERN (these 16 rows form pattern)

Row 1 (RS): p3, k4, p2, k2, p2, k4, p3
Row 2: k3, p4, k2, p2, k2, p4, k3
Rows 3–8: Rep Rows 1 and 2, 3x more
Row 9: p3, C4F, p2, k2, p2, C4B, p3
Row 10: same as Row 2
Row 11: p3, k2, C4F, k2, C4B, k2, p3
Row 12: k3, p14, k3
Row 13: p3, k4, p1, T2F, T2B, p1, k4, p3
Row 14: same as Row 2
Row 15: same as Row 1
Row 16: same as Row 2

BACK

CO 77 (85, 91, 97) sts.

Next row: * k1, p1; rep from * to last st, k1. Work 1x1 rib until piece measures 1.5" working 5 inc across last WS row, 82 (90, 96, 102) sts.

Set up patt as foll:

Row 1 (RS): k10 (13, 15, 17), pm, work 20 st cable panel, pm, k22 (24, 26, 28), pm, work 20 st cable panel, pm, k10 (13, 15, 17).

Row 2: p10 (13, 15, 17), slip marker, work 20 st cable panel, slip marker, p22 (24, 26, 28), slip marker, work 20 st cable panel, slip marker, p10 (13, 15, 17).

Tip: After you've knit Rows 1 and 2 above, you will start knitting from the 16 pattern rows. Note, however, that the stitches listed in the pattern rows only apply to the 2 sets of 20 stitches between the markers. For all other stitches, you will knit on the right side of the work and purl on the wrong side to form stockinette stitch.

TIPS

- In order to keep the continuity of the pattern, it is crucial to keep track of which row you are knitting. Get a row counter (see page 9) and use it.
- You can only bind off at the beginning of the row. (See pages 50–51 for information on how to bind off.) You will have to knit 4 rows to bind off 2 stitches on each side 2 times.
- To make sure that your increases slant in the direction of the armhole shaping, do a k2togtbl or ssk decrease on the right side of the piece and a k2tog decrease on the left side.

Cont working Rows 1–16 of 20 st cable panel between markers on a background of st st until piece measures 11.5" (12.5", 14.5", 15").

ARMHOLE SHAPING

Keeping continuity of patt, BO 2 sts each side 2x. Dec 1 st each side every other row 3x (4x, 4x, 5x), 68 (74, 80, 84) sts. Work until piece measures 19.5" (21", 23", 24").

NECK SHAPING

Keeping continuity of patt, work 23 (25, 27, 28) sts, place next 22 (24, 26, 28) sts on a holder, add another ball of yarn, work last 23 (25, 27, 28) sts. BO 2 sts each neck edge 1x, 21 (23, 25, 26) sts. Work until piece measures 20.5" (22", 24", 25"). Place shoulder sts on holder.

Tip: To add another ball of yarn, simply put down the first ball (do not cut the yarn) and start knitting the stitches after the holder with the new ball. Leave a 10- or 12-inch tail for seaming. You will work only the 2 sets of 23 (25, 27, 28) stitches on either side of the holder. Leave the 22 (24, 26, 28) stitches on the holder alone. You will pick up these stitches later when you work the neck binding.

FRONT

Work as for back until piece measures 15.5" (16.5", 18.5", 19").

Tip: You will work the front to 11.5 (12.5, 14.5, 15) inches and then do the armhole shaping as above. Continue on these 68 (74, 80, 84) stitches until the piece measures 15.5 inches and then work the neck shaping below.

NECK SHAPING

Work 31 (34, 37, 39) sts, k2tog, k1, add another ball of yarn, k1, ssk, k31 (34, 37, 39). Cont in patt, dec 1 st each neck edge every other row until 21 (23, 25, 26) sts rem. Work until piece measures 20.5" (22", 24", 25").

FINISHING

Knit shoulder seams together.

Tip: See the Skill Workshop on pages 70–71 for instructions on how to knit the shoulder seams together.

NECK BINDING

PU and k22 (24, 24, 26) sts from left shoulder seam to center v, m1 at center v, pu and k22 (24, 24, 26) sts to shoulder seam, pu and k5 sts to back holder, k22 (24, 26, 28) sts from holder, pu and k6 sts to shoulder seam. PM.

Tip: If you haven't already been using one, you will need to switch to a circular needle to work the neck and armhole bindings (you could also use a set of double pointed needles). You will pick up the 2 sets of 22 (24, 24, 26) stitches along both sides of the front neck edges as well as the extra 11 stitches you will pick up on either side of the back holder (5 on the right side and 6 on the left). Be sure to space these stitches evenly. See pages 68–69 for details on how to pick up stitches.

Rnd 1: [k1, p1] to center st, knit center st, [p1, k1] to last st, p1.

Rnd 2: [k1, p1] to last 2 sts before center st, ssk, knit center st, k2tog, [p1, k1] to last st, p1.

Rnd 3: [k1, p1] to last 3 sts before center st, k1, p2tog, knit center st, p2togtbl, [k1, p1] to end.

BO loosely in rib.

ARMHOLE BINDINGS

PU and k85 (89, 89, 93) sts around armhole opening. Work 1x1 rib for 3 rows. BO loosely in rib.

Sew side seams together.

Cables are a distinctive pattern, seen often in traditional Aran knitting. Cables are created by twisting a group of stitches over another group of stitches, by placing the stitches to be twisted on a separate needle designed for the purpose. Cables are crossed from left to right (a left cable) or from right to left (a right cable) and can contain groups of two, three, or more stitches. Left twists are followed by right twists in the pattern to give the cable its distinctive twining look.

To twist a 4-stitch cable to the left:

Two stitches slipped purlwise onto cable needle

1. On a right-side row of a swatch, work to the position where you want to place the first cable.

2. Slip the next 2 stitches, as if to purl them, onto the cable needle.

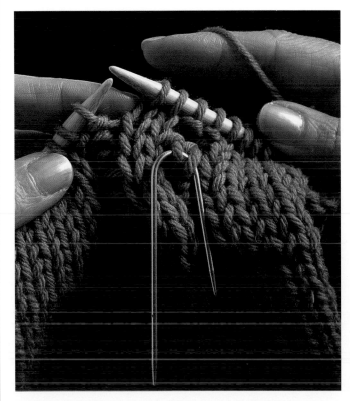

3. Holding the cable needle at the front, knit the next 2 stitches in the row with the cable needle holding the 2 slipped stitches still at the front.

Seattle Bound Vest

4. Return the 2 stitches on the cable needle to the left needle, slipping them one by one.

5. Knit the returned stitches as usual.

6. Repeat this pattern as often as is specified in the pattern. Use a stitch counter to keep track of rows.

To twist a 4-stitch cable to the right, follow Steps 1–2 above, but instead of holding the cable needle at the front, hold it at the back. Then, as you did with Steps 3–5 above, knit the next 2 stitches in the row with the cable needle at the back and then return the 2 stitches on the cable needle to the left needle and knit them. Repeat this pattern as often as is specified in the pattern. Use a stitch counter to keep track of rows.

Cable twisted to the right

Cable twisted to the left

The completed cable pattern

8

Bamboo Forest Sweater

Gauge: 18 sts and 34 rows to 4" in patt on US 9 needles or size to obtain gauge

Finished Bust Measurement: [28 (33, 36)"] [41.25 (44, 46.5, 49.25, 52)"]

Length: [16.5 (18, 19)"] [20.5 (21, 22, 23, 25)"]

NOTE: The first set of brackets are children's sizes.

Materials:

Wool in the Woods Gypsy (100% Cotton), [4 (5, 6)] [7 (8, 8, 9, 10)] skeins

US 8 and US 9 Needles (or size to obtain gauge)

5 Stitch Holders (2 6-inch, 3 4¹/₂-inch)

This project introduces a simple but fascinating technique known as slip-stitch knitting.

When used with just one skein of yarn (either solid or variegated in color) slip-stitch knitting produces a visually interesting basket-weave texture. As you will learn in the Skill Workshop, however, this technique can also be used to great effect when you add a second skein of yarn in a different color. Once you perfect the slip-stitch technique with a single skein with the sweater, you can then move on to more complex applications with two skeins.

99

PATTERN (these 4 rows form pattern)

Row 1 (RS): * p3, sl1 wyif, k1, sl1 wyif; rep from * to last 3 sts, p3.

Rows 2 and 4: * k3, p3; rep from * to last 3 sts, k3.

Row 3: * p3, k1, sl1 wyif, k1; rep from * to last 3 sts, p3.

BACK

With larger needles, CO [69 (75, 81)] [93 (99, 105, 111, 117)] sts. Work 3 x 3 rib for 4 rows. Beg patt on RS and work until piece measures [9 (10, 10.5)"] [11 (11.5, 12, 13, 14)"].

ARMHOLE SHAPING

BO 2 sts each armhole edge [1x] [2x]. Dec 1 st each armhole edge every other row [4x] [4x], [57 (63, 69)] [77 (83, 89, 95, 101)] sts. Cont in patt until piece measures [15.5 (17, 18)"] [19.5 (20, 21, 22, 24)"].

TIPS

- In order to keep the continuity of the pattern, it is crucial to keep track of which row you are knitting. Get a row counter (see page 9) and use it.
- You can only bind off at the beginning of the row. (See pages 50–51 for information on how to bind off.) You will have to knit 4 rows to bind off 2 stitches on each armhole edge 2 times.
- To make sure that your increases slant in the direction of the armhole shaping, do a k2togtbl or ssk decrease on the right side of the piece and a k2tog decrease on the left side.

NECK SHAPING

Work [19 (21, 23)] [24 (26, 28, 30, 32)] sts, place next [19 (21, 23)] [29 (31, 33, 35, 37)] sts on a holder, add another ball of yarn and work last [19 (21, 23)] [24 (26, 28, 30, 32)] sts. BO 2 sts each neck edge 1x, [17 (19, 21)] [22 (24, 26, 28, 30)] sts. Cont until piece measures [16.5 (18, 19)"] [20.5 (21, 22, 23, 25)"].

Place shoulder sts on holders.

Tip: To add another ball of yarn, simply put down the first ball (do not cut the yarn) and start knitting the stitches after the holder with the new ball. Leave a 10- or 12-inch tail for seaming. You will work only the 2 sets of [19 (21, 23)] [24 (26, 28, 30, 32)] stitches on either side of the holder. Leave the [19 (21, 23)] [29 (31, 33, 35, 37)] stitches on the holder alone. You will pick up these stitches later when you work the neck binding.

FRONT

Work as for back until piece measures [14 (15.25, 16.25)"] [17.5 (18, 18, 19, 21)"].

Tip: You will work the front to [9 (10, 10.5)"] [11 (11.5, 12, 13, 14)"] and then do the armhole shaping as above. Continue on these [57 (63, 69)] [77 (83, 89, 95, 101)] stitches until the piece measures [15.5 (17, 18)"] [19.5 (20, 21, 22, 24)"] and then work the neck shaping below.

NECK SHAPING

Work [23 (25, 27)] [29 (31, 33, 35, 37)] sts, place next [11 (13, 15)] [19 (21, 23, 25, 27)] sts on a holder, add another ball of yarn and work last [23 (25, 27)] [29 (31, 33, 35, 37)] sts. Working both sides together, BO 2 sts each neck edge 2x. Dec 1 st each neck edge every other row [2x] [3x] , [17 (19, 21)] [22 (24, 26, 28, 30)] sts. Cont until piece measures [16.5 (18, 19)"] [20.5 (21, 22, 23, 25)"].

SLEEVES (working both sleeves tog)

With larger needles, CO [27 (33, 39)] [39] st. Work 3 x 3 rib for 4 rows. Beg patt and at the same time, keeping continuity of pattern, inc 1 st each side every 4th row to [69 (73, 77)] [77 (77, 77, 77, 79)] sts.

Tip: "Working both sleeves together" means that you will cast on two separate sets of [27 (33, 39)] [39] stitches with two separate balls of yarn. Follow the instructions for both sleeves. This will ensure that both sleeves end up the same length.

Adult Sizes Only: Inc 1 st each side every 6th row to [85 (85, 85, 85, 89)] sts.

Work until sleeves measure [14 (15.5, 16.75)"] [17 (17, 18, 18, 19)"].

CAP SHAPING

BO 2 sts each side [1x] [2x]. Dec 1 st each side every other row 4x. BO 5 sts [3x] [4x]. BO 6 sts each side [0 (1, 2)x] [2x]. BO remaining sts loosely.

FINISHING

Knit shoulder seams together. Sew in sleeves. Sew up side seams.

Tip: See pages 70–71 for instructions on how to knit shoulder seams together. Refer to the illustration of the Teddy Bear Sweater assembly on page 56 for hints on sewing in the sleeves.

NECK BINDING

With smaller needles, pu and k [14 (14, 15)] [16 (16, 18, 18, 18)] sts from left shoulder seam to front holder, k [11 (13, 15)] [19 (21, 23, 25, 27)] sts from holder, pu and k [14 (14, 15)] [16 (16, 18, 18, 18)] sts to shoulder seam, pu and k5 sts to back holder, k [19 (21, 23)] [29 (31, 33, 35, 37)] sts from holder, pu and k5 sts to shoulder seam. PM and purl 1 row. BO loosely in knit.

Tip: If you haven't already been using one, you will need to switch to a circular needle to work the neck binding. You will pick up [14 (14, 15)] [16 (16, 18, 18, 18)] on the left side of the front holder, then knit the [11 (13, 15)] [19 (21, 23, 25, 27)] stitches from the front holder. You will then pick up [14 (14, 15)] [16 (16, 18, 18, 18)] stitches on the right side of the front holder, 5 stitches on the right side of the back holder, and then knit the [19 (21, 23)] [29 (31, 33, 35, 37)] stitches from the back holder. You will finish by picking up 5 stitches on the left side of the back holder. Be sure to space the picked up stitches evenly. See pages 68–69 for details on how to pick up stitches.

SKILL WORKSHOP: SLIP STITCH KNITTING

The basic technique for slip stitch knitting is the same whether you use it with one skein of yarn or two. The instructions that follow will teach you how to bring forward a second color of yarn, but the technique can be applied the same way when using just one color. If you are working in just one color of yarn (or variegated yarn from the same skein, as is the case with the Bamboo Forest Sweater), skip Step 1 and start with Step 2. You will create the same horizontal bars in your garment, but they will appear in the same color yarn as the rest of the stitches in the garment.

3. Slip the next stitch as if to purl.

1. Join the new color (see pages 44–45) and knit across the row to the point you want to bring forward the old color (in this case, the old color is blue and the new color is yellow).

2. Bring the working yarn to the front of the work.

4. Return the working yarn to the back of the work.

5. Knit the next stitch in the row as usual.

6. As you can see, this creates a horizontal bar at the bottom of the slipped stitch in the new color, while the stitch itself is in the old color.

To slip a stitch with the horizontal bar visible on the wrong side of the work:

1. Keeping the working yarn to the back of the work, slip the next stitch as if to purl.

Barbara Walker's Knitting Legacy

The mosaic knitting technique was first introduced by Barbara G. Walker, a landmark knitter known as well today for her books on feminism, mythology, and folklore. See the Resources section on page 119 for publication details of several of her books on knitting.

2. Knit the next stitch in the row as usual.

3. There is no horizontal bar at the base of the slipped stitch, but a bar in the new color is visible at the base of the slipped stitch on the wrong side of the work.

9

Honeybee Tea Cozy

Gauge: 11 sts and 12 rows to 4" on US 15 needles or size to obtain gauge

Finished Measurements:

Height: 9.5"

Width: 17" at bottom of cozy

Materials:

Wool in the Woods Star City Wool
(100% Wool, 200 yds/skein)

Hay (Color A): 2 skeins

Honey (Color B): 2 skeins

24" Circular US 15 Needles
(or size to obtain gauge)

This project introduces a simple but versatile technique known as felting. Felting is a method by which you can produce wool-fabric garments or accessories by knitting a piece loosely with wool yarn and then shrinking it to obtain the size and texture of felt. Like most felting projects, the Honeybee Tea Cozy is worked on large needles and therefore knits up fairly quickly. As you will see in the Skill Workshop, the felting process itself takes only a few hours but requires an extended period for shaping and drying.

PATTERN (these 16 rows form pattern)

Rnds 1–4: With Color A, knit.

Rnds 5 and 7: With Color A, * k4, sl1, [k5, sl1] to last 4 sts, k4 *, sl marker, work from * to * 1x more.

Rnds 6 and 8: With Color A, * p4, sl1, [p5, sl1] to last 4 sts, p4 *, sl marker, work from * to * 1x more.

Rnds 9–16: As Rows 1–8 with Color B.

COZY

With Color A, CO 138 sts. PM and join. K69, pm, k69. Work 16 rows patt.

Keep continuity of patt throughout dec rnds.

Work dec rnd as follows: k2togtbl, work to 2 sts before marker, k2tog, sl marker, k2togtbl, work to 2 sts before marker, k2tog. Work Rows 2–8 even (134 sts).

Tip: An ssk can be substituted for the k2togtbl—see page 41.

Work dec rnd. Work Rows 10–16 even (130 sts).

Work dec rnd. Work rnd 2. Work dec rnd. Work rnd 4. Work rnds 5–8 even (122 sts).

Work dec rnd. Work rnd 10. Work dec rnd. Work rnd 12. Work rnds 13–16 even (114 sts).

Work dec rnd. Work rnd 2. Work dec rnd. Work rnd 4. Work dec rnd. Work rnd 6. Work rnds 7–8 even (102 sts).

Work dec rnd. Work rnd 10. Work dec rnd. Work rnd 12. Work dec rnd. Work rnd 14. Work dec rnd. Work rnd 16 (86 sts).

Work double dec rnd as follows: k2togtbl 2x, work to 4 sts before marker, k2tog 2x, sl marker, k2togtbl 2x, work to 4 sts before marker, k2tog 2x. Work rnd 2. Work double dec rnd. Work rnd 4. Work double dec rnd. Work rnd 6. Work double dec rnd. Work rnd 8 (54 sts).

Turn tea cozy inside out. Place 27 sts on spare needle. Work 3 needle BO on 27 sts from spare needle and 27 sts from working needle.

Tip: See pages 70–71 for instructions on how to work the 3-needle Bind Off.

FINISHING

Fold tea cozy in half; with Color B, work 3 st attached I-cord through both pieces of fabric, picking up 1 st in each gar st ridge along sides, and 1 st in each st along top of tea cozy; at the same time at center top, work 5" unattached I-cord.

TIPS

- See page 77 for instructions on how to work I-cord.
- Don't forget to work the unattached 5-inch I-cord at the same time you work the attached I-cord.

With Color A, work attached I-cord, picking up 1 st in each st along CO row around. Using tapestry needle, weave I-cord ends together.

FELTING

Tip: See the Skill Workshop on pages 106–7 for more information on felting.

Place cozy in a laundry bag or pillow protector. Wash in regular cycle with detergent in hot water, checking often. You may need to run an additional wash cycle, as washers vary. Remove before spin cycle. Shape and stand to dry.

Optional: Add bumblebee buttons for adornment.

Before felting a knitted garment you will need to have first knit it to the exact specifications of the pattern. Yarn choice is integral to successful felting; only 100% wool will felt properly, so be sure to purchase the type of yarn recommended in the pattern.

Note: When felting, you will need access to a washing machine with hot water.

To felt a finished knitted piece:

2. Place the pillowcase in the washer.

1. Place the finished piece to be felted in an old pillowcase. Knot the end of the pillowcase loosely (or close the zipper if it has one) to keep the piece inside. This will protect your washing machine from excess wool lint.

Tip: Very hot water works best when felting. If your hot water heater is kept on a lower setting (to save energy or because of small children in your home), you may want to either turn it up temporarily (be sure to warn other members of the household first) or use someone else's washing machine.

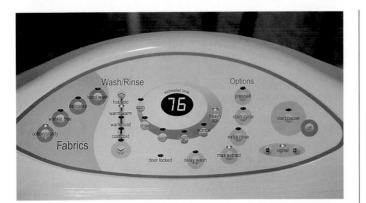

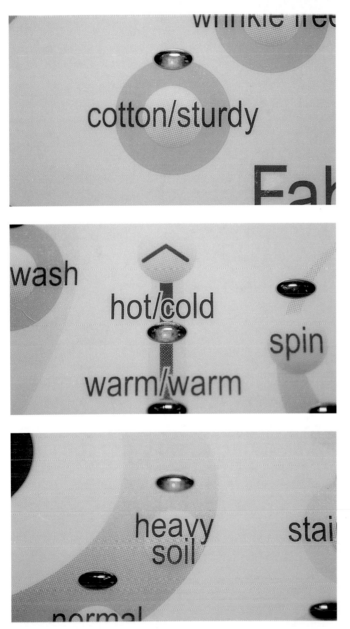

Tip: Washing machines' settings will vary. The two most important are that the water is hot and that the wash cycle is long. You will need to experiment with the settings on your own washer to see which produce the best results.

4. Turn on the washing machine and let it run through the wash cycle. Check on the item after about 5 minutes and every 5 minutes or so after that. Different yarns felt at different rates. Washing machine variations also will affect the total felting time. Checking frequently will prevent the piece from overshrinking. If you are reaching the end of the cycle and the piece is still not the right size, turn the settings for the wash cycle back a few minutes to allow for additional wash time. Do not allow the washer to start the rinse and spin cycle—this can cause too much shrinkage or permanently crease the felt.

5. Once the felted piece has reached the proper size, remove it from the hot water with tongs or a wooden spoon. Remove it from the pillowcase, and rinse it well in cool water. Press the water out of it with a large towel. Do not wring it. For some pieces such as hats, blocking will be required to set the piece in its final shape as it dries. Your pattern will give more detailed instructions on blocking techniques.

3. Set the washer to a hot wash/cold rinse, on the cotton/sturdy cycle, and on heavy soil (or any other setting that will lengthen the time of the wash cycle). You only need enough water to submerge the pillowcase, so if your washer has a water level option, set it to the lowest setting. Add a very small amount of laundry detergent and close the lid.

10

Comfort in Diamonds Throw

Gauge: 6.5" x 6.5" = 1 block on US 11 needle or size to obtain gauge

NOTE: It will be necessary to knit a complete block to accurately check gauge.

Finished Measurements: 54" x 61"

Materials:

Wool in the Woods Pop (Cotton/Rayon blend, 200 yds/skein) 9 skeins, Natural

Wool in the Woods Frolic (100% Rayon, 200 yds/skein) 9 skeins, Multi

US 11 Needle (or size to obtain gauge)

Crochet Hook (size K)

NOTE: Hold one strand of Pop and one strand of Frolic together throughout the throw.

Although this final project in the book may be the most time-consuming, it is certainly not the most complicated. On the contrary, once you learn how to knit the basic block, you will simply continue to knit the blocks in numerical order as designated in the diagram, picking up and casting on new stitches along the edges to create the next block in the sequence. As you will learn in the skill workshop, the combination of the two different types of yarn will produce the throw's rich texture. You can experiment with this technique in other projects that you try on your own.

BLOCK 1: WORK 6, SINGLY

Using long tail method, CO 35 sts loosely.

    Row 1 (WS): k17, p1, k17

    Row 2: k16, S2KP2, k16

    Row 3: k16, p1, k16

    Row 4: Knit to 1 st before center st, S2KP2, knit to end

    Row 5: Knit to center st, p1, knit to end

    Rows 6–33: Rep Rows 4 and 5

    Row 34: S2KP2

Tip: S2KP2: Slip 2 stitches together as if to knit 2 together, knit next stitch, pass 2 slipped stitches over knit stitch.

Tip: When creating the throw, it helps to think of each block as having a lettered side. Refer to this diagram in the Tip boxes throughout the pattern

Tip: When knitting blocks in numerical sequence, it will not be necessary to fasten off the yarn for each block. You may continue to pick up stitches for next block with the same yarn. This will reduce the number of ends to be woven into the throw.

BLOCKS 2, 4, 8, 14, 22

Foll diagram, pu 17 sts along Side B of the corresponding Block 1 in the bottom row, turn work, using cable CO, CO 1 st, turn work, pu 17 sts along Side A of the next Block 1 in bottom row.

    Rows 1–34: Follow Block 1

Tip: For example, when working Block 2, pu 17 sts along Side B of 1st Block 1, CO 1 st, then pu 17 sts along Side A of 2nd Block 1; when working Block 4, pu 17 sts along Side B of 2nd Block 1, CO 1 st, then pu 17 sts along Side A of 3rd Block 1.

BLOCKS 5, 6, 9, 10, 11, 12, 15, 16, 17, 18, 19, 20, 23, 24, 25, 26, 27, 28, 29, 30, 33, 34, 35, 36, 37, 38, 39, 40, 42, 43, 44, 45, 46, 47, 49, 50, 51, 52, 54, 55

Foll diagram, pu 17 sts along Side A of corresponding block in row below, pu 1 st in center st of block below, pu 17 sts along Side B of block in row below.

    Rows 1–34: Follow Block 1

Knitting by Number

You will begin by knitting 6 of Block 1. They will form the bottom row of the throw and anchor all the other blocks. From there you will continue to knit blocks in numerical sequence (2, 3, 4, 5, 6, etc.) until you complete Block 56. The throw will grow from the lower left corner upwards, each diagonal row of blocks picking up stitches from the previous row. Be sure to follow the pattern instructions for how individual blocks need to be constructed. Once you have completed Block 56, you will finish the throw by adding the 10 triangles along the edges.

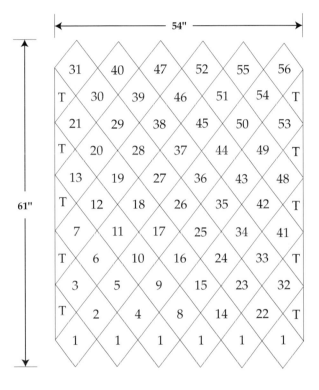

Tip: For example, when working Block 5, pu 17 sts along Side A of Block 4, pu 1 st in center st of 2nd Block 1 in bottom row, then pu 17 sts along Side B of Block 2; when working Block 6, pu 17 sts along Side A of Block 5, pu 1 st in center st of Block 2, then pu 17 sts along Side B of Block 3.

BLOCKS 3, 7, 13, 21, 31

Foll diagram, pu 17 sts along Side A of corresponding block in row below, pu 1 st in center st of block below, turn work, using cable CO, CO 17 sts for Side D of block.

    Rows 1–34: Follow Block 1

Tip: For example, when working Block 3, pu 17 sts along Side A of Block 2, pu 1 st in center of 1st Block 1 in bottom row, turn work, then CO 17 sts to form Side D of Block 3; when working Block 7, pu 17 sts along Side A of Block 6, pu 1 st in center of Block 3, turn work, then CO 17 sts to form Side D of Block 7.

BLOCKS 32, 41, 48, 53, 56

Foll diagram, using long tail CO, CO 17 sts for Side C of block, pu 1 st in center st of block below, pu 17 sts along Side B of block in row below.

Rows 1–34: Follow Block 1

Tip: For example, when working Block 32, CO 17 sts to form Side C of Block 32, pu 1 st in center of 6th Block 1 in bottom row, then pu 17 sts along Side B of Block 22; when working Block 41, CO 17 sts to form Side C of Block 41, pu 1 st in center of Block 32, then pu 17 sts along Side B of Block 33.

TRIANGLES

Foll diagram, work 5 along each side of throw to produce straight edges.

For triangles on left side of throw:

Foll diagram, pu 17 sts along Side A of corresponding block below, pu 1 st under center st where two blocks join (placing stitch under will keep continuity of center ridge), pu 17 sts along Side D of block above.

For triangles on right side of throw:

Pu 17 sts along Side B of block below, pu 1 st under center st where two blocks join (placing stitch under will keep continuity of center ridge), pu 17 sts along Side C of block above.

Row 1 (WS): k17, p1, k17
Row 2: ssk, k14, S2KP2, k14, k2tog
Row 3: k15, p1, k15
Row 4: ssk, knit to 1 st before center st, S2KP2, knit to last 2 sts, k2tog
Row 5: Knit to center st, p1, knit to end
Rows 6–15: Rep Rows 4 and 5
Row 16: S2KP2

Tip: For example, when working bottom left triangle, pu 17 sts along Side A of 1st Block 1, pu 1 st under center of where Block 3 and 1st Block 1 join, then pu 17 sts along Side D of Block 3. When working bottom right triangle, pu 17 sts along Side B of 6th Block 1, pu 1 st under center of where Block 32 and 6th Block 1 join, then pu 17 sts along Side C of Block 32.

FINISHING

Using crochet hook, 1 st in from side edge, work sl st chain through each row of knitted fabric. This will mimic center ridge of blocks in throw.

Tip: See the Skill Workshop on page 112 for instructions on how to work a slip stitch chain edge.

One of the simplest ways to create an exciting texture or color combinations in a project is by knitting with two different skeins of yarn. As you did in the Bay Side Scarf (page 61), you simply hold both strands together as you knit with them. But unlike in the scarf, where the yarns were both the same weight and texture, more unusual results can be achieved by combining yarns of varying weights, textures, and colors. Match a delicate mohair with a more substantial DK weight, or combine a novelty eyelash with a slubby cotton. You can experiment with these combinations in the simple garter stitch scarves that have recently become popular.

Here are a couple other combinations to consider:

A solid mohair combined with a variegated boucle produces this wonderful texture.

A metallic-thread novelty yarn combined with a variegated spiral yarn creates this interesting color pattern.

Comfort in Diamonds Throw

Other than running in the ends when you are finished with the throw, the only other finishing technique you will need to apply to this project will be creating a slip stitch chain along both straight edges of the throw. This crocheted edge will mimic the center ridge between the internal blocks of the throw and give the piece a more uniform look.

Making a slip stitch chain edge is simple:

Note: The example below is worked on a single triangle, substituting bright yellow cotton yarn for the natural Pop rayon/cotton blend in order to make the slip stitch chain edge easier to see.

1. Starting on the right side of the bottom of the throw and working upwards, insert the crochet hook down into the center of the first stitch, 1 stitch in from the edge. Make a loop of yarn around the hook, leaving a 3-inch tail to be worked through later.

2. Pull the loop up through the stitch to the front of the work.

3. With the first loop still on the hook, insert the hook down into the next stitch and pull another loop through. You will now have two loops on the hook.

4. Continue pulling the second loop through the first loop so there is now one loop on the hook.

5. Repeat Steps 3 and 4 until you have worked all the stitches along the right edge. Repeat Steps 1–5 along the left edge of the throw.

A slip stitch chain edge

Appendices

Knitting Abbreviations Master List

Following is a list of knitting abbreviations used by yarn industry designers and publishers. The most commonly used abbreviations are highlighted. In addition, designers and publishers may use special abbreviations in a pattern, which you might not find on this list. Generally, a definition of special abbreviations is given at the beginning of a book or pattern.

Abbreviation	Description
[]	work instructions within brackets as many times as directed
( )	work instructions within parentheses in the place directed
* *	repeat instructions following the asterisks as directed
*	repeat instructions following the single asterisk as directed
"	inch(es)
alt	alternate
approx	approximately
beg	begin/beginning
bet	between
BO	bind off
CA	color A
CB	color B
CC	contrasting color
cm	centimeter(s)
cn	cable needle
CO	cast on
cont	continue
dec	decrease/decreases/decreasing
dpn	double pointed needle(s)
fl	front loop(s)
foll	follow/follows/following
g	gram
inc	increase/increases/increasing
k or **K**	knit
k2tog	knit 2 stitches together
kwise	knitwise
LH	left hand
lp(s)	loop(s)
m	meter(s)
M1	make one—an increase—several increases can be described as "M1"
M1 p-st	make one purl stitch
MC	main color
mm	millimeter(s)
oz	ounce(s)
p or **P**	purl

Abbreviation	Description
pat(s) or **patt**	pattern(s)
pm	place marker
pop	popcorn
p2tog	purl 2 stitches together
prev	previous
psso	pass slipped stitch over
pwise	purlwise
rem	remain/remaining
rep	repeat(s)
rev St st	reverse stockinette stitch
RH	right hand
rnd(s)	round(s)
RS	right side
sk	skip
skp	slip, knit, pass stitch over—one stitch decreased
sk2p	slip 1, knit 2 together, pass slip stitch over the knit 2 together; 2 stitches have been decreased
sl	slip
sl1k	slip 1 knitwise
sl1p	slip 1 purlwise
sl st	slip stitch(es)
ss	slip stitch (Canadian)
ssk	slip, slip, knit these 2 stitches together—a decrease
sssk	slip, slip, slip, knit 3 stitches together
st(s)	stitch(es)
St st	stockinette stitch/stocking stitch
tbl	through back loop
tog	together
WS	wrong side
wyib	with yarn in back
wyif	with yarn in front
yd(s)	yard(s)
yfwd	yarn forward
yo	yarn over
yrn	yarn around needle
yon	yarn over needle

Skill Levels for Knitting

SKILL LEVELS FOR KNITTING

1	■□□□	**Beginner**	Projects for first-time knitters using basic knit and purl stitches. Minimal shaping.
2	■■□□	**Easy**	Projects using basic stitches, repetitive stitch patterns, simple color changes, and simple shaping and finishing.
3	■■■□	**Intermediate**	Projects with a variety of stitches, such as basic cables and lace, simple intarsia, double pointed needles and knitting in the round needle techniques, mid-level shaping and finishing.
4	■■■■	**Experienced**	Projects using advanced techniques and stitches, such as short rows, fair isle, more intricate intarsia, cables, lace patterns, and numerous color changes.

Appendices courtesy of the Craft Yarn Council of America www.yarnstandards.com

Most crochet and knitting pattern instructions will provide general sizing information, such as the chest or bust measurements of a completed garment. Many patterns also include detailed schematics or line drawings. These drawings show specific garment measurements (bust/chest, neckline, back, waist, sleeve length, etc.) in all the different pattern sizes. To ensure proper fit, always review all of the sizing information provided in a pattern before you begin.

Following are several sizing charts. These charts show Chest, Center Back Neck-to-Cuff, Back Waist Length, Cross Back, and Sleeve Length **actual body measurements** for babies, children, women, and men. These measurements are given in both inches and centimeters.

When sizing sweaters, the fit is based on actual chest/bust measurements, plus ease (additional inches or centimeters). The first chart entitled "Fit" recommends the amount of ease to add to body measurements if you prefer a close-fitting garment, an oversized garment, or something in-between.

The next charts provide average lengths for children's, women's, and men's garments.

Both the Fit and Length charts are simply guidelines. For individual body differences, changes can be made in body and sleeve lengths when appropriate. However, consideration must be given to the project pattern. Certain sizing changes may alter the appearance of a garment.

HOW TO MEASURE

1. Chest/Bust
Measure around the fullest part of the chest/bust. Do not draw the tape too tightly.

2. Center Back Neck–to–Cuff
With arm slightly bent, measure from back base of neck across shoulder around bend of elbow to wrist.

3. Back Waist Length
Measure from the most prominent bone at base of neck to the natural waistline.

4. Cross Back
Measure from shoulder to shoulder.

5. Sleeve Length
With arm slightly bent, measure from armpit to cuff.

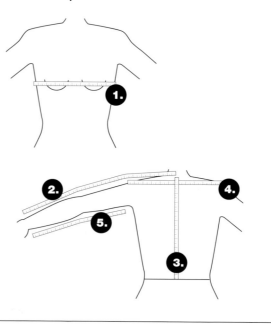

FIT

Very-close fitting: Actual chest/bust measurement or less
Close-fitting: 1–2"/2.5–5cm
Standard-fitting: 2–4"/5–10cm
Loose-fitting: 4–6"/10–15cm
Oversized: 6"/15cm or more

LENGTH FOR CHILDREN

Waist length: Actual body measurement
Hip length: 2"/5cm down from waist
Tunic length: 6"/15cm down from waist

LENGTH FOR WOMEN

Waist length: Actual body measurement
Hip length: 6"/15cm down from waist
Tunic length: 11"/28cm down from waist

LENGTH FOR MEN

Men's length usually varies only 1–2"/ 2.5–5cm from the actual "back hip length" measurement (*see chart*)

Baby's size	3 months	6 months	12 months	18 months	24 months
1. Chest (in.)	16	17	18	19	20
(cm.)	*40.5*	*43*	*45.5*	*48*	*50.5*
2. Center Back Neck-to-Cuff	10½	11½	12½	14	18
	26.5	*29*	*31.5*	*35.5*	*45.5*
3. Back Waist Length	6	7	7½	8	8½
	15.5	*17.5*	*19*	*20.5*	*21.5*
4. Cross Back (Shoulder to shoulder)	7¼	7¾	8¼	8½	8¾
	18.5	*19.5*	*21*	*21.5*	*22*
5. Sleeve length to Underarm	6	6½	7½	8	8½
	15.5	*16.5*	*19*	*20.5*	*21.5*

Child's size	2	4	6	8	10
1. Chest (in.)	21	23	25	26½	28
(cm.)	*53*	*58.5*	*63.5*	*67*	*71*
2. Center Back Neck-to-Cuff	18	19½	20½	22	24
	45.5	*49.5*	*52*	*56*	*61*
3. Back Waist Length	8½	9½	10½	12½	14
	21.5	*24*	*26.5*	*31.5*	*35.5*
4. Cross Back (Shoulder to shoulder)	9¼	9¾	10¼	10¾	11¼
	23.5	*25*	*26*	*27*	*28.5*
5. Sleeve length to Underarm	8½	10½	11½	12½	13½
	21.5	*26.5*	*29*	*31.5*	*34.5*

Standard Body Measurements/Sizing continued

Child's (cont.)	12	14	16
1. Chest (in.)	30	31½	32½
(cm.)	76	80	82.5
2. Center Back Neck-to-Cuff	26	27	28
	66	68.5	71
3. Back Waist Length	15	15½	16
	38	39.5	40.5
4. Cross Back (Shoulder to Shoulder)	12	12¼	13
	30.5	31	33
5. Sleeve Length to Underarm	15	16	16½
	38	40.5	42

Woman's size	X-Small	Small	Medium	Large
1. Bust (in.)	28–30	32–34	36–38	40–42
(cm.)	71–76	81–86	91.5–96.5	101.5–106.5
2. Center Back Neck-to-Cuff	27–27½	28–28½	29–29½	30–30½
	68.5–70	71–72.5	73.5–75	76–77.5
3. Back Waist Length	16½	17	17¼	17½
	42	43	43.5	44.5
4. Cross Back (Shoulder to Shoulder)	14–14½	14½–15	16–16½	17–17½
	35.5–37	37–38	40.5–42	43–44.5
5. Sleeve Length to Underarm	16½	17	17	17½
	42	43	43	44.5

Woman's (cont.)	1X	2X	3X	4X	5X
1. Bust (in.)	44–46	48–50	52–54	56–58	60–62
(cm.)	111.5–117	122–127	132–137	142–147	152–158
2. Center Back Neck-to-Cuff	31–31½	31½–32	32½–33	32½–33	33–33½
	78.5–80	80–81.5	82.5–84	82.5–84	84–85
3. Back Waist Length	17¾	18	18	18½	18½
	45	45.5	45.5	47	47
4. Cross Back (Shoulder to Shoulder)	17½	18	18	18½	18½
	44.5	45.5	45.5	47	47
5. Sleeve Length to Underarm	17½	18	18	18½	18½
	44.5	45.5	45.5	47	47

Standard Body Measurements/Sizing continued

Man's Size	Small	Medium	Large	X-Large	XX-Large
1. Chest (in.)	34–36	38–40	42–44	46–48	50–52
(cm.)	*86–91.5*	*96.5–101.5*	*106.5–111.5*	*116.5–122*	*127–132*
2. Center Back Neck-to-Cuff	32–32½	33–33½	34–34½	35–35½	36 36½
	81–82.5	*83.5–85*	*86.5–87.5*	*89–90*	*91.5–92.5*
3. Back Hip Length	25–25½	26½–26¾	27–27¼	27½–27¾	28–28½
	63.5–64.5	*67.5–68*	*68.5–69*	*69.5–70.5*	*71–72.5*
4. Cross Back (Shoulder to Shoulder)	15½–16	16½–17	17½–18	18–18½	18½–19
	39.5–40.5	*42–43*	*44.5–45.5*	*45.5–47*	*47–48*
5. Sleeve Length to Underarm	18	18½	19½	20	20½
	45.5	*47*	*49.5*	*50.5*	*52*

Head Circumference Chart

	Infant/Child				Adult	
	Premie	**Baby**	**Toddler**	**Child**	**Woman**	**Man**
6. Circumference						
(in.)	12	14	16	18	20	22
(cm.)	*30.5*	*35.5*	*40.5*	*45.5*	*50.5*	*56*

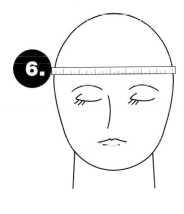

For an accurate head measure, place a tape measure across the forehead and measure around the full circumference of the head. Keep the tape snug for accurate results.

Standard Yarn Weight System

Categories of yarn, gauge ranges, and recommended needle and hook sizes

Yarn Weight Symbol & Category Names	1 Super Fine	2 Fine	3 Light	4 Medium	5 Bulky	6 Super Bulky
Type of Yarns in Category	Sock, Fingering, Baby	Sport, Baby	DK, Light Worsted	Worsted, Afghan, Aran	Chunky, Craft, Rug	Bulky, Roving
Knit Gauge Range* in Stockinette Stitch to 4 inches	27–32 sts	23–26 sts	21–24 sts	16–20 sts	12–15 sts	6–11 sts
Recommended Needle in Metric Size Range	2.25–3.25 mm	3.25–3.75 mm	3.75–4.5 mm	4.5–5.5 mm	5.5–8 mm	8 mm and larger
Recommended Needle U.S. Size Range	1 to 3	3 to 5	5 to 7	7 to 9	9 to 11	11 and larger
Crochet Gauge* Ranges in Single Crochet to 4 inch	21–32 sts	16–20 sts	12–17 sts	11–14 sts	8–11 sts	5–9 sts
Recommended Hook in Metric Size Range	2.25–3.5 mm	3.5–4.5 mm	4.5–5.5 mm	5.5–6.5 mm	6.5–9 mm	9 mm and larger
Recommended Hook U.S. Size Range	B–1 to E–4	E–4 to 7	7 to I–9	I–9 to K–10½	K–10½ to M–13	M–13 and larger

* GUIDELINES ONLY: The above reflect the most commonly used gauges and needle or hook sizes for specific yarn categories.

Resources

BOOKS

Bliss, Debbie. *How to Knit*. North Pomfret, VT: Trafalgar Square, 1999.

Square, Vicki. *The Knitters Companion*. Loveland, CO: Interweave Press, 1996.

Swansen, Meg. *Handknitting With Meg Swansen*. Pittsville, WI: Schoolhouse Press, 1995.

———. *Meg Swansen's Knitting*. Loveland, CO: Interweave Press, 1999.

Vogue Knitting Magazine Editors. *Vogue Knitting: The Ultimate Knitting Book*. Rev. ed. New York: SoHo Publishing Co., 2002.

Walker, Barbara. *Charted Knitting Designs: A Third Treasury of Knitting Patterns*. Pittsville, WI: Schoolhouse Press, 1998.

———. *A Fourth Treasury of Knitting Patterns*. Pittsville, WI: Schoolhouse Press, 2000.

———. *Mosaic Knitting*. Pittsville, WI: Schoolhouse Press, 1997.

———. *A Second Treasury of Knitting Patterns*. Pittsville, WI: Schoolhouse Press, 1998.

———. *A Treasury of Knitting Patterns*. Pittsville, WI: Schoolhouse Press, 1998.

Zimmerman, Elizabeth. *Elizabeth Zimmerman's Knitter's Almanac*. Mineola, NY: Dover Publications, 1985.

———. *Elizabeth Zimmerman's Knitting Workshop*. Pittsville, WI: Schoolhouse Press, 1981.

———. *Knitting Around*. Pittsville, WI: Schoolhouse Press, 1989.

———. *Knitting Without Tears: Basic Techniques and Easy-to-Follow Directions for Garments to Fit All Sizes*. New York: Simon and Schuster, 1973.

YARN AND KNITTING SUPPLIES

One of the true joys of knitting is finding a good local yarn shop and establishing a relationship with the people who work there. Knitting store employees are almost always knitters themselves and can serve as an invaluable resource, especially for beginners. Most urban areas have at least one good yarn shop. Check your local telephone directory. You can also refer to the wonderful online list compiled at *www.woolworks.org* to find knitting stores in your area.

If you are not fortunate enough to live near a local yarn shop, there are several good online resources and catalogs that you can use. There are hundreds of such retail outlets available on the internet; just a few are mentioned here. Use a search engine such as *www.google.com* to find others.

NOTE: Some online retailers also have brick and mortar stores. Where applicable, a street address is provided.

eKnitting.com
800-438-5464
www.eknitting.com

Halcyon Yarn
12 School Street
Bath, ME 04530
800-341-0282
www.halcyonyarn.com

Kaleidoscope Yarns
15 Pearl Street
Essex Junction, VT 05452
802-288-9200
www.kaleidoscopeyarns.com

Needles!
56 Union Street South
Concord, NC 28025
704-789-8928
www.jklneedles.com

Patternworks
36 South Gate Drive
P. O. Box 1690
Poughkeepsie, NY 12601
800-438-5464
www.patternworks.com

Schoolhouse Press (books and yarn)
800-968-5648
www.schoolhousepress.com

Worldknit.com, Inc.
218-824-5648
www.worldknit.com

ONLINE RESOURCES FOR KNITTERS

ChicKnits
A fun and useful collection of tips, patterns, and links as well as the author's knitting blog.
www.chicknits.com

Craft Yarn Council of America
The craft yarn industry's trade association website with wonderful educational links and free projects. Link to downloadable version of the Standards and Guidelines for Crochet and Knitting.
www.craftyarncouncil.com

Interweave Press
Publisher of *Interweave Knits* magazine and many great knitting books. Website contains back issues and pattern errata as well as links to knitting charities and other information.
www.interweave.com

Knitty
A delightful new quarterly web-only knitting magazine with articles, columns, and patterns.
www.knitty.com

The Knitting Guild of America
The national association for hand knitters and publisher of *Cast On* magazine. Website contains membership information and a link to the magazine.
www.tkga.com

The Knitting Pages
An online collection of patterns, corrections, reviews, and knitting charts, as well as a list of yarn shops and a list of links.
www.knittingpages.com

The Knitting Universe
Online site for *Knitter's Magazine* and XRX Books. Pattern errata and back issues as well as a online forums and mailing list.
www.knittinguniverse.com

Knitter's Review
An online magazine with extensive yarn and book review archives as well as patterns and discussion boards.
www.knittersreview.com

Vogue Knitting
Publisher of *Vogue Knitting* magazine and many great knitting books. Site includes corrections as well as online access to the current issue of the magazine.
www.vogueknitting.com

Woolworks
The oldest and one of the best collections of hand-knitting information on the internet. A great directory of knitting stores around the world.
www.woolworks.org

Yarn Information

Special thanks to Carol Woolcock at The Mannings for donating the Jaggerspun Zephyr, to Skacel for donating the Merino Light #11, and to Cascade Yarns for donating the Cascade 220. All other yarn featured in finished projects was provided by Wool in the Woods. See the information below for details on how to obtain this yarn.

Jaggerspun Zephyr (used in Bay Side Scarf, page 61)
Visit *www.jaggeryarn.com* to find a yarn shop near you.

Skacel Merino Light (used throughout the Basic Skills
    section and in the Seattle Bound Vest, page 94)
Visit *www.skacelknitting.com* to find a yarn shop near
    you.

Cascade Yarns Cascade 220 (used in Northwest Ridge
    Hat, page 72 and Mittens, page 89)
Visit *www.cascadeyarns.com* to find a yarn shop near
    you.

Wool in the Woods
Terrain (used in the Biscayne Bay Shell, page 66)
Twin Twist (used in the 2 x 2 Socks, page 78)
Gypsy (used in the Bamboo Forest Sweater, page 99)
Star City Wool (used in the Honeybee Tea Cozy,
    page 104)
Pop (used in the Comfort in Diamonds Throw,
    page 108)
Frolic (used in the Comfort in Diamonds Throw,
    page 108)
Visit *www.woolinthewoods.com* to find a yarn shop near
    you or for ordering information.